RAISING RESPECTFUL CHILDREN

in a Disrespectful World

JILL RIGBY

HOWARD BOOKS
A DIVISION OF SIMON & SCHUSTER, INC.
NEW YORK   NASHVILLE   LONDON   TORONTO   SYDNEY   NEW DELHI

Howard Books
A Division of Simon & Schuster, Inc.
1230 Avenue of the Americas
New York, NY 10020

This Howard Books trade paperback edition August 2013

HOWARD and colophon are trademarks of Simon & Schuster, Inc.

For information about special discounts for bulk purchases, please contact Simon & Schuster Special Sales at 1-866-506-1949 or business@simonandschuster.com.

The Simon & Schuster Speakers Bureau can bring authors to your live event. For more information or to book an event, contact the Simon & Schuster Speakers Bureau at 1-866-248-3049 or visit our website at www.simonspeakers.com.

Designed by Davina Mock-Maniscalco

Manufactured in the United States of America

10   9   8   7   6   5   4   3   2   1

Library of Congress Cataloging-in-Publication Data
Rigby, Jill M.
    Raising respectful children in a disrespectful world / Jill Rigby.
        p. cm.
    Includes bibliographical references.
    1. Child rearing. 2. Parenting. 3. Moral development. 4. Respect. 5. Mass media and children.
I. Title.
    HQ769.R554 2006
    649'.7—dc22

                                                                        200604357

ISBN 978-1-4767-1878-1
ISBN 978-1-4165-4257-5 (ebook)

To Chad and Boyce, my grown sons.
And Elise, my new daughter.

Chad, the time has come for you to lead a family
of your own with humble confidence.

Elise, I couldn't have picked a more perfect helpmate for my son.

Boyce, enjoy your solitude. It won't last forever.

Contents

Acknowledgments

I MUST BEGIN WITH my husband, Nick Garner. For any who took the time to read these acknowledgments in the first edition, you'll know there was not a husband to acknowledge. After fifteen years of singlehood, God, in His great love and mercy, brought the most wonderful man into my life who never seems to grow weary of his wife's foolish ways. He is encouraging, ever-loving, and ever-forgiving, and I must say, cooks the best grilled burgers in town.

Mother, now eighty-four and still going strong. Still inspiring and growing in grace.

Daddy, whose influence continues to linger in my heart and writing. This world could sure use his no-nonsense approach to life . . . right is right and wrong is wrong.

Coach Payton Jordan became a legend with his passing in 2009. How thankful I am for the time I was able to visit with him. His commitment to excellence and integrity will live on in the hearts of the boys he built into men.

Jean Rohloff held my hand through the first writing. In this edition, her amazing words, found in "After the Storm," bring this book to a close.

Donna Munson, my big sister in Christ, continues to walk through life with me. It was her gift of "Be Satisfied with Me" that brought me into a deeper relationship with our heavenly Father.

Mike and Lisa Conn, more than lifelong friends. You've stood by me through the trials and struggles of life. It is an honor to share the story of you and your girls. I welcome your words of wisdom to these pages.

Wilbur and Betsy Mills share their amazing story of raising four children for almost nine years in remote parts of Brazil during a tour of mission duty. I wrote about their son Wil's extraordinary artistic gifts, developed in those years of imagination-building in the jungle. Wil has since passed to heaven, but his poetic words will stay with us.

The staff of Manners of the Heart®: Debbie, Lori, and Karis, who not only helped with research and brainstorming, but allowed me to disappear to write the revisions. I'm so proud to say, they didn't need me . . . but I sure do need them.

What would we do without the best interns in the world, Jessie, Sam, and Melissa? In one way or another, you each contributed to the completion of the revisions.

Steve Laube, I can't believe you're still there for me. I've been absorbed in writing curricula, not books, for the last four years, but you have continued offering advice and a listening ear.

Philis, you're the most patient editor in the industry. Your continued belief in the mission of Manners of the Heart and your willingness to champion our cause means the world to me.

Robert and Mary, Sally and Rich, and Burton—you all welcomed me into your family. Your precious little ones, Garett, Jack, Allie, and Alston, inspire me to keep going when I face discouragement. GG is doing all I can to make this world a better place for you.

Always, to the Manners of the Heart Board members, parents, teachers, volunteers, and businesses who share my passion and support our efforts to bring a return of respect and civility to our country.

Last and most important, the Manners of the Heart kids who love Wilbur and embrace his teaching. I believe with my whole heart that your generation will become the "Rebuilders" who will repair the damage done by mine.

With deepest gratitude,
I love you all

Foreword

WHAT AN HONOR to be a special part of a journey that we all as parents must travel. Like many of you who pick up this book, I am a lot of things to many people; wife, daughter, executive, cheerleader, chef, taxi driver, friend—the list goes on, but my most coveted, treasured, and completely terrifying role is Mom. Failure is not an option. Job performance is critical. There is never a day off. Training is on-the-job and there are always new challenges. Children do not come with how-to manuals and each is unique, a one-of-a-kind model. We do, however, have one overriding all-encompassing tool in our parenting tool box—our love. We have an overwhelming desire to guide our children to become all that they are destined to become.

If there were a perfect recipe for raising children, we would all be eating the same thing for breakfast, lunch, and dinner. In this high-tech, high-stress, time-crunched world, where information is at our finger tips and instantaneous gratification is expected, it's time to focus on the simple and the long term. We make it so complicated because we think that if it were really simple all children would be perfectly perfect in every way. Jill's amazing insight and dedication to raising respectful children in a disrespectful world engages that simple golden rule: treat others the way you wish to be treated. She affirms that your actions have a positive or negative impact, and we can choose how we act—it's a decision. The empowerment you bestow upon your children when you teach them the value of their impact is immeasurable.

Speaking of recipes, for meals in my house I often felt like a short order cook. For breakfast, Ashleigh wanted pancakes, Lindsey wanted yogurt, Aaron wanted eggs, and Camryn wanted a bowl of oatmeal. I often wanted to blend it all together and serve it up shake style! I was catering to their wants and worn out by 6:30 a.m. I first met Jill after such a morning. I was taking a moment out of my busy day to find out more about a new program called Manners of the Heart, which their school was integrating into classrooms. In all honesty, I almost skipped the meeting; my schedule was pretty tight. I don't believe in coincidences—I was meant to hear that message. It took Jill just five minutes and one visual to hugely influence the direction of my parenting. I have four great kids—smart, engaging, happy, and yes, even respectful. I felt confident that I was preparing my children to lead truly impactful lives. I know, I know, it sounds awfully hokey—how could a program aimed at kindergarten through fifth grade could change the course of my parenting role? After all, like I said, my kids were pretty great already, why mess with a good thing?

It was the mirror that got me (don't skip ahead to pages 24–25!). My (at the time) two-, four-, six-, and eight-year-olds were headed straight down a path that nurtured self-esteem. I was in praise mode, "You're smart, you're pretty, you're a great little baseball player, and you are such a wonderful dancer!" I am embarrassed to admit that my six-year-old had slippers with the slogan, "It's all about me" on the toes! In that moment I knew it was important to my children's future to fundamentally begin changing their perception of who they were and why they were important to the world. In fact, it changed my perception of myself as the person I would want my children to become. They still know that they are smart and pretty and great athletes, but that is secondary to their sphere of influence, the lives they touch, and their positive influence on others.

Nothing is more important to me than raising respectful children. I want to know their hearts, offer encouragement, allow failure, and celebrate their accomplishments. It transcends being polite (which is expected). This parenting thing is a journey. When my oldest was in her teens (and that's a parenting conundrum!), we had a discussion about the easy road or the hard road, about being average or being "You," and about making a difference. No matter how wonderful your children are, those teenage years are an exercise in patience and perseverance. I have no doubt that the simple life lessons and concepts throughout the first edition of *Manners of the Heart* and *Raising Respectful Children in a Disrespectful World* were my true North, the reality of my impact on guiding the four most amazing people in my world to adulthood.

Fast forward twelve years, with two children now in university pursuing their dreams and two in high school still lovingly challenging me every day. There is never a dull moment at the Holub home (although breakfast is much simpler). The continuous roller coaster of life, the dips, turns, and overall rush has made for some interesting times and a wonderful sense of peace, joy, and accomplishment. My greatest wish for you the reader is to have your own "aha" moment, to look through the window, see your reflection, and realize the impact and blessing of you in our world and with your own child(ren).

Jill's *Raising Respectful Children in a Disrespectful World* is just what we all need to feed our parenting souls and the perfect "cookbook filled with recipes" for those hungry (and picky) children. So get cooking!

—Sandra MacKellar Holub
executive director, the Albemarle Foundation,
privileged to be the mom of Ashleigh,
Lindsey, Aaron, and Camryn Holub

Preface

ANOTHER STORM HAS come.

On August 29, 2005, as I was working fast and furiously to complete the final manuscript of *Raising Respectful Children in a Disrespectful World,* Hurricane Katrina raged out of the Gulf of Mexico onto the coast of Louisiana. The devastation was unprecedented. No one was prepared to meet the acute needs of thousands of our citizens who were left homeless in an instant.

Homes were demolished. Lives were destroyed.

Tens of thousands fled from New Orleans to Baton Rouge. Every square foot of space was opened as shelter for the displaced victims. Towels, blankets, and clothing were gathered from across the region. Every cast-iron gumbo pot in Louisiana was fired up to feed hungry bellies.

We did the best we could.

Manners of the Heart launched "Project: To My Friend" to help children connect with other children. We delivered hundreds of backpacks, school supplies, and letters of hope from children across the globe to children living in chaos.

Days passed. Weeks passed. Months turned into years.

Some of the wounded returned to their old lives and made them better. Many found new lives filled with hope and promise. Others chose to remain stuck in the mud.

Today, August 29, 2012, the winds are kicking up. The rains are coming down. As I write, the worst of Hurricane Isaac is upon us. After it passes, will we return to our old lives? Will we be forced to start new lives? Will the storm leave us just as it found us?

How extraordinary it is to be revising the same book during Isaac that I was writing during the historic Katrina! I can't help but wonder if there is a reason for this strange "coincidence."

I believe there is.

The theory presented in *Raising Respectful Children in a Disrespectful World* seven years ago was that the self-esteem movement had darn near destroyed our children and our society. Evidence of a society gone awry was offered to substantiate that premise and help was given to prevent future damage to the next generation of children.

Just as the hurricanes have continued to rage across my home state, the violent storm of self-esteem has continued blowing its fierce winds of destruction through our society. I continue to sound the warning signal, begging folks to listen. To wake up. To hear the message of Manners of the Heart. Many have listened and found help for recovery, but still . . .

Homes are being decimated. Lives are being destroyed. Children are suffering.

I'm convinced this book is more relevant today than when it was first published. The goal of every parent to raise respectful children who become respectable adults has never been more difficult to achieve, but the obstacles we face in that quest have never been more obvious. Understanding where the disrespectfulness in our culture comes from will equip you to handle it. My hope is that parents, far and wide, will read this information, embrace it, and transform their homes for the sake of their precious children.

The time to rebuild is now . . . after the storm.

Jill Rigby Garner
Baton Rouge, Louisiana
August 30, 2012

Introduction

A CLASSIC TOMBOY STOOD in front of me. Long burnished hair with rippling waves fell on her shoulders, looking unwashed and unkempt. Suzie's eyes looked away, then down, as she stood at the table. But never into mine.

She was one of many kids being interviewed for a special study we were conducting among children ages four to fourteen. Taller than most, she stooped to avoid towering over the other girls.

Halfway through the survey, I asked a question that revealed her pain: "What's the nicest thing your parents could ever say to you? What would really make your heart feel good?"

"Be a lady."

Her answer confused me. Why would she want her parents to tell her to be a lady? Her demeanor proclaimed she was anything but. I saw no indication that this was her deepest desire. As I'd watched her enter the room, I suspected Suzie was angry, but I didn't know why.

So I asked her, "Do you usually listen to your parents?"

Her reply was an abrupt and emphatic "No!"

"Why not?"

She leaned over the table to make her point, looking directly in my eyes. "Because I'm in rebellion."

"What are you rebelling against?"

"I've already told you!"

Wiggling in my seat, I tried to remember answers she had already given. I knew that Suzie desperately needed to know I had been listening to her. She didn't need another adult who seemed not to care enough to pay attention.

"Let me see, Suzie," I muttered, stalling.

When I looked up at her, she gave me a look of disgust, as if to say, "Don't you get it?"

I got it. Her stance gave it away. "You're rebelling because you really want to be a lady and nobody's helping you. Is that it?"

She nodded her head as she shifted hips and re-crossed her arms. "Yeah."

I was looking at the face of rebellion. Suzie wasn't angry about what was right; she was angry about what was wrong.

I suspect she's like many other kids on this score. Today's kids are angry and rebellious at rates higher than those of any other generation. They are the first generation to do worse psychologically, socially, and economically than their parents. But they're not rebelling against rigidity and rules, as the hippies of the sixties did; they are rebelling against the lack of structure and adult guidance.

At a much deeper level, today's kids are seeking revenge. The adults in their lives say one thing and live another, and the kids see through their parents' phoniness, lack of direction, and insecurities. These kids want to get even. They're lashing out at a society that has not given them what they really need . . . security within boundaries. They want to inflict on others the pain that has been inflicted on them. What they can't see is that their revenge will destroy them.

Our children, from ghettos to gated communities, are desperate, searching for someone who will tell them the truth.

You, parent, should be that person.

Suzie desperately wants someone to teach her how to be a lady. She doesn't want to be an angry, insecure, awkward girl. She wants to become a confident young woman, but no one seems to care or even notice, so she's going to scream until someone does. Not with an audible scream, but with an insidious moaning from the depths of her soul.

As the next group of kids came to the table, Suzie turned to leave, but I couldn't let her just walk away. "Suzie, I need a hug. It's been a long morning."

She hesitated but walked back when I stretched open my arms and added, "You're the only one tall enough around here to hug me." As we embraced, I whispered in her ear, "Be a lady, the beautiful lady that I see inside." Her lips quivered, but I can't say I saw a smile.

I'm hoping and praying that Suzie's parents will wake up and help her. If they don't, I'm afraid that within two years their daughter's rebellion will only intensify, and she'll end up hurting both those around her and herself.

You picked up this book because you want to raise respectful children in today's disrespectful world. This is an achievable goal, and you can succeed, even if at the moment it seems like an impossible task. To do so, you must be willing to:

+ Be the person you want your children to become

+ Abandon old notions of building self-esteem, and enroll your family in the School of Respect

+ Help your children find their purpose and use perseverance to fulfill that purpose

✦ Use encouragement to motivate your children, not praise

✦ Set boundaries without building walls between you and your children

✦ Use discipline to instill goodness in your children

✦ Do all you can to protect and shield your children from the garbage of our culture

✦ Engage your children in meaningful activities, not useless entertainment

✦ Find contentment so your children can be filled with gratefulness

✦ Listen with your heart to your children's needs

Not sure you can do it?

I know you can ... if you follow God's principles. His principles are so broad that they transcend both culture and time, yet so practical that they will equip you with every tool needed to train your children in manners of the heart.

With this revised edition, we have added features to help you receive the greatest benefit from this book:

✦ Each chapter opens with an introduction outlining the inevitable aftermath of self-esteem related to the chapter topic.

✦ "A Personal Note to Single Parents" has been expanded to make room for "the rest of the story."

✦ The "Must-Read Books" section has been revised with additional suggestions.

✦ For individuals or small groups, a Study Guide has been

included in the back of the book to help you put into practice the principles presented.

Throughout the book you'll find quotes from Wise Ol' Wilbur, the voice of wisdom at Manners of the Heart. Wilbur lives in the only Happle Tree in the world in a little town called Merryville that rests between the Mountains and the Sea. Children are introduced to Wilbur and his companions, Peter and Penelope raccoons, Buddy and Bully bulldogs, Sketch the Skunk, BillyBeeRight, and a host of other characters, as they learn how to become respectful citizens of their communities.

I invite you to come with me (and Wise Ol' Wilbur) and explore how you can help undo the damage in today's children from a culture gone awry. It is my honor to be your guide as you raise respectful children in the midst of our disrespectful world.

1

What Went Wrong?

D AYS PASSED. WEEKS passed. Months turned into years. The winds kept blowing.

We have been loving ourselves, believing in ourselves, esteeming ourselves, and teaching our children to do the same. Look at the devastation left behind:

+ A mortgage meltdown was brought about by folks who bought more than they could afford because they believed they should have it anyway.

+ Sports heroes are stripped of their titles because they choose to use performance-enhancing drugs to avoid defeat and ensure their victories.

+ Twenty-somethings, incapable of taking care of themselves, are returning home to be taken care of by someone else.

✦ One in four marriages among baby boomers in their fifties are ending in divorce because they're looking for happiness.[1]

✦ On a reality TV show, a girl planning her sixteenth birthday party wants a major road blocked off so a marching band can precede her grand entrance on a red carpet.

These are examples of the aftermath of self-esteem—two generations drowning in narcissism.

The danger signs were right in front of our noses. For more than ten years, Manners of the Heart has been sounding the alarm, trying to convince our society that if we do not take shelter from the storm, we will suffer the consequences. We saw what the inevitable outcome of self-esteem would be from our immersion in the day-to-day work of helping parents raise children and teachers teach children who were lost in themselves, either self-conceited or self-conscious.

Why did anyone ever think that raising children to believe in themselves, love themselves, and esteem themselves would lead to anything but narcissism?

Jean Twenge, author of *The Narcissism Epidemic*, notes, "In trying to build a society that celebrates high self-esteem, self-expression, and 'loving yourself,' Americans have inadvertently created more narcissists—and a culture that brings out the narcissistic behavior in all of us."[2]

In this chapter, you will find there is a window of hope. If we raise the present generation to believe in *others*, love *others*, and esteem *others*, this generation can recover from the damage of self-esteem and lead a restoration of respect that can rebuild our society.

✷ ✷ ✷

WHEN I WAS GROWING UP, people weren't perfect, but society was certainly more civil. The line between right and wrong was clear. There was a sense of law and order.

Teachers were teachers. So teachers taught.

Parents were parents. So parents parented.

Kids were kids. So kids obeyed.

Respect for authority was paramount. Service to others and respect for property were natural elements of community. Teaching manners and instilling character were the cornerstones of public education. Parents looked at the right side of the report card (conduct) before they looked at the left (grades). Kids got in a lot more trouble if they were disrespectful to a teacher than if they made a B minus.

Times past weren't perfect, but there certainly was an attitude of respectfulness that's now missing.

Today we live in a society where:

✦ A high school valedictorian chose to use profanity in her graduation address, even in the presence of young children. And to make matters worse, her father supported her decision to "stand her ground" when she was asked to apologize and refused.

✦ Incessant texting takes place at the family dinner table, in classrooms, in boardrooms, while driving, and even during face-to-face conversations.

✦ Foul language is used in public, not only by males in the presence of females, but by females in the presence of males.

I could fill this book with one example after another of disrespectful behavior. How did this happen? How did our respectful world become so disrespectful? We substituted self-esteem for self-respect, and in the process we lost our manners.

We Replaced Self-Respect with Self-Esteem

MORE THAN TWENTY YEARS AGO when I began visiting my twin sons' school cafeteria to teach table manners, I had no concept that a volunteer project for a local school would grow into a full character education program that is now being used in schools and homes across the country. Since then, *Manners of the Heart* (a curriculum for schools) and *Manners of the Heart at Home* (a parents' guide to the school curriculum) have been changing the lives of children, families, and communities.

My experience of working with children and parents has convinced me that the troubles of today can be traced back to the early seventies, when a group of psychologists began theorizing why the rebellion of the sixties had taken place. Some experts concluded that the fifties were a time of such rigidity that teenagers who grew up in the "era of rules" were destined to revolt.

The overwhelming majority of professionals, however, agreed that the reason teenagers rebelled was because of a deep need to be someone—not just an American, but an individual. Not a member of a corporate body, but an individual making his or her own decisions based on personal beliefs, not the beliefs of parents or society. "Believe in yourself" became the mantra of the day.

Specialists began telling parents the secret to raising healthy children was to build their self-esteem. Books on the subject of self-esteem skyrocketed to the top of bestseller lists, encouraging parents to be friends, not authority figures, with their kids. Discipline was out. Experts said that children needed to make their own decisions. Slowly but surely, children became the center of the universe.

Parents today are still being told that the secret to raising healthy children is to build their self-esteem—praise 'em in the morning, praise 'em at the noontime, praise 'em when the sun goes down. We've been told to never deny our children anything and to stand against anyone who dares to correct our little ones—all with the goal of helping our kids feel good about themselves.

I received the following letter from parents who did all they were told to do in raising their fourteen-year-old son:

> He has very low self-esteem and very little motivation or desire to succeed in play or academics. We try to use positive reinforcement and praise him for completing projects or whatever we see him do well or put effort into. We make a point not to compare him to other children, but he tries hard to be like others (*he really doesn't know what he likes or even who he is*). He is in trouble at school almost every day for disrespect, and we know that he can do better . . . he just needs to know that he *can*, and he has to want to try to do better. Please help! Any suggestions?

These parents had followed the advice of the day. But rather than help their son, they had unwittingly hurt him.

One of my favorite no-nonsense parenting experts, John Rosemond, agrees that by emphasizing self-esteem, we've lost something of great value:

> Character development has been de-emphasized and psychological development has become the focus. As this babble rose to a din, our collective perceptions of children began to change. We began to view them not as fairly durable

little people who needed to be taught respect, responsibility, good manners, and the like, but as fragile little containers of something called self-esteem, which could be irreparably damaged with a harsh word.[3]

As a result of this emphasis on self-esteem, twenty-somethings are returning home rather than facing the world on their own. College kids are flunking out because they don't know how to manage their schedules. Kids are growing up without problem-solving skills because their parents think love means solving all their problems for them. Many adolescents have no respect for authority because their parents didn't command their respect. Instead, these parents gave too much and expected too little.

In our attempt to build self-esteem in children, we have reared a generation of young people who are failing at life, haven't a clue who they are, and are struggling to find a reason for living. These kids fall for the latest craze, healthy or unhealthy. It doesn't matter, as long as they're in the middle of it. They would rather die than give up their cell phones. And they feel that others have an obligation to serve them.

Roy F. Baumeister, professor of psychology at Florida State University, was a proponent of self-esteem in the early seventies but has since changed his views. Forty years later, Baumeister now recommends, "Forget about self-esteem and concentrate more on self-control and self-discipline. Recent work suggests this would be good for the individual and good for society—and might even be able to fill some of those promises that self-esteem once made but could not keep."[4] I agree. Rather than seeking to build self-esteem in our children, we need to focus on building self-control and self-discipline, which will develop self-respect.

Many people use the words *self-esteem* and *self-respect* synonymously, but I believe the two are worlds apart. When we seek to help kids feel good about themselves (the goal of self-esteem), we teach them to focus on *themselves* and how *they* feel and what *they* want. I believe this perspective keeps children from participating in the world; it encourages them to see everything as if looking into a mirror, so they grow up believing "it's all about me."

Kids raised with a focus on self-esteem have an unbalanced view of the world. They live by the motto "I want it, and I want it now." Kids with this attitude aren't exhibiting self-confidence. They are exhibiting self-conceit, a view of themselves that says they are superior to others.

But when we help kids respect themselves, we teach them to focus on *others*, and how *others* feel and what *others* need. This perspective, in turn, leads children to see everything through a window, seeing their own images reflected against the world beyond the glass, rather than in a mirror, and to grow up believing "it's more about others and less about me."

So what's the bottom-line difference between self-esteem and self-respect? Self-esteem is "me centered," while self-respect is "others centered."

The quest for self-esteem has turned the world upside down. Shifting to the pursuit of self-respect will turn the world right-side up again. Why? Because kids with self-respect put others ahead of themselves. They feel an obligation to others and a responsibility to society. Bullies can't rock their foundation, because kids who have self-respect know who they are and what they stand for. They have a balanced view of the world. Their confidence is balanced with humility; they exhibit humble confidence.

> **Self-respect** is the fruit of discipline; the sense of dignity grows with the ability to say no to oneself.
>
> —Abraham J. Heschel

If you are parenting to build self-respect in your children, you'll focus on who your kids are becoming rather than on how much you give them. You'll teach them how to serve others rather than to expect to be served. You'll teach them to contribute to the world rather than to expect the world to give to them. You'll teach your kids to do their best, whether that means being number one or not, and to work toward goals so they can experience the satisfaction and confidence that a job well done brings.

Let's sum up the different results of these two parenting goals:

Self-Esteem	Self-Respect
Happiness (which is fleeting)	Joy (which is lasting)
Greed	Gratitude
Arrogance	Obedience
Insecurity	Confidence
Discontentment	Contentment
Futility	Perseverance
Self-centeredness	Others-centeredness
Ill-mannered	Well-mannered

The result of parenting to build self-esteem? Undisciplined, rude, greedy, disrespectful, and ill-mannered children. The result of parenting to develop self-respect? Disciplined, caring, productive, respectful, and well-mannered children.

Unfortunately, because our society for the past four decades has emphasized self-esteem rather than self-respect in kids, we have far more disrespectful children than respectful children. Consequently, old-fashioned courtesies are considered unimportant, and we've lost our moral foundation.

We Lost Our Manners and Therefore Lost Our Morals

TODAY, IT'S THE RARE CHILD who says:

"Please."

"May I help you?"

"Yes Sir" and "Yes Ma'am." (Yes, I'm from the Deep South. Frankly, I wish the rest of the country would follow us on this one. There is no better vehicle for teaching young children respect than through the use of "Sir" and "Ma'am.")

"May I get your chair?"

"Excuse me."

"Thank you."

"I'm sorry."

In the quest for self-esteem, such courtesies have become uncommon, at least among the members of the new royalty. Little kings and queens are not expected to humble themselves before others by extending common courtesies.

Judith Martin, better known as the syndicated columnist "Miss Manners," offers this insightful explanation of the critical importance of manners:

The attitude that the wishes of others do not matter is exactly what manners are intended to counter. And no one has yet come up with a satisfactory substitute for family etiquette training in the earliest years of life to foster the development of the child in such principles of manners as consideration, cooperation, loyalty, respect. . . . As a result of the ever-wider abandonment of home etiquette training, schools have become increasingly stymied by problems they identify as lack of discipline and commitment to moral behavior. . . . A society can hope to function virtuously only when it also recognizes the legitimacy of manners.[5]

Respect lies at the heart of manners and morals. A person's respect for authority, respect for others, and respect for self go a long way toward determining the moral decisions that person makes. Manners instilled in the early years become the foundation for moral behavior in the later years.

> *Respect* for ourselves guides our morals; respect for others guides our manners.
> —Laurence Sterne

Scripture affirms the relationship of morals and manners—the content of the heart (morals) is the basis for outward behavior:

The good man brings good things out of the good stored up in his heart, and the evil man brings evil things out of the evil stored up in his heart. For out of the overflow of his heart his mouth speaks.[6]

Good people do good things because of the good in their hearts. Bad people do bad things because of the evil in their hearts. Your words show what is in your heart.[7]

It's who you are, not what you say and do, that counts. Your true being brims over into true words and deeds.[8]

In other words, the respectful child produces good deeds from a good heart, and a disrespectful child produces bad deeds from a corrupted heart. Whatever is in your child's heart determines what your child will say and do.

If you want to raise respectful children in a disrespectful world, you must command their respect through a balance of love and discipline, especially in the little things. When it comes to working with kids, the little things *are* the big things. And the younger the child, the more important the little things. Raising respectful children requires loving your child enough to not give in to the indulgent request of the moment. It means loving your child enough to stop what you're doing to fully listen. When your children respect you, they will more easily respect God, and in the process respect others and themselves.

Is it possible to fill the hearts of our children with the "right stuff"? Can we raise respectful children in a disrespectful world? You'd better believe it. It's not as hard as you might think. It just takes spiritual muscle and emotional fortitude. Both are within reach, if you know where to turn.

The next generation is ready for the absolute truth. They want and need the world to be turned right-side up again. It's our duty to develop the spiritual muscle needed to help them.

Your Charge

JESUS ASKED THE FATHER NOT to take His disciples out of the world, but to protect them from the evil in the world.[9] Our charge as parents is to prepare our children to be *in* the world and not *of* the world. We must train them to stand on their own two feet. With loving guidance, our children can affect the world without becoming infected by it.

You can equip your children with humble confidence so they can handle whatever comes at them. It's not your children's minds that will help them do that, but their hearts.

Let the disrespectful world blow its fierce winds. You *can still* raise respectful children in this disrespectful world who will be able to withstand the onslaught of the storm.

2

Where Have All the Parents Gone?

OUR NATION WATCHED in horror during hurricanes Katrina and Rita as folks spent days in attics across the Gulf Coast waiting for rescue. Thousands believed they could "ride out the storm," as they had so many storms before. Tens of thousands opted to ignore the warnings. Thousands more were caught unprepared.

More than four hundred thousand people were evacuated to more than forty states. Parents were separated from children. Children were separated from parents. Reuniting 5,192 children with their parents became the largest child-recovery effort in U.S. history.[1]

During the days of rescue and the months that followed, blame was thrown everywhere. Neighbors blamed neighbors for looking out for themselves but not one another. Folks blamed the government for not responding quickly enough. Parents blamed the authorities for not having a better evacuation plan. Regardless of who was to blame for what, in the end, each individual had to take responsibility for his or her own choices, good and bad. Casting blame did not help the recovery process; it only delayed it.

Unfortunately, it's not only during storms that blame is thrown around when children become lost, separated from their families. When children become disrespectful and out-of-control, we want to blame the narcissistic culture for the disrespectful attitudes of our children. But we as parents are the first responders; therefore, if blame is to be put anywhere, it must be placed on our shoulders.

Abandonment doesn't happen only when a parent leaves the home; children are too often abandoned by parents living under the same roof. Parents bury their children in stuff to avoid giving up their own time on their personal pursuits. They relinquish their parental authority by saying yes, because yes is easier than the hard work of saying no. Each member of the family lives in a separate room in the house in a relationship with an electronic box.

And we wonder why children have such disrespectful attitudes?

In this chapter, you'll be given three parenting choices. If you choose to accept blame where blame is due, you can guide your family through the torrential rains and become their hero! Your children are counting on you to make the right choice so you can help them grow up to become the respectful, responsible young adults they are meant to be.

How well your children (and your family) weather the storm depends on you.

* * *

MY EYES COULDN'T FIND THEIR way back to the pages of my book because my heart was tied to the image on the TV screen. A teenage girl stood in the middle of an empty street in the early morning hours, looking more like a prostitute than a lost child. Smoke from her cigarette swirled around her face. An investigative reporter stepped into the frame to begin his interview.

"How long have you been on the streets?" he questioned.

The coldness of her heart poured out in her words as she revealed that she had been on the streets for five years, since the age of eleven.

What could possibly have driven her to the streets at eleven years old? I wondered. Why have her parents not come to her rescue? Are they dead?

The reporter continued his conversation with the displaced teenager. "You don't want to live like this, do you? Don't you want out of this existence?"

For a moment her shoulders fell and the hardness in her eyes softened. Looking beyond the reporter into the obscurity of the street, she replied with a broken whisper, "Yeah . . . but I can't find the door."

While this teenager's situation may be extreme, far too many children, even those living at home with their parents, are "unable to find the door." In a less dramatic but no less damaging way, these kids are raising themselves. Journalist David Brooks agrees. He visited several high schools a decade ago, spending time with students, listening to their dreams and listening to their hearts. He reported his conclusions in an article for the *Atlantic Monthly*. Here is an excerpt from that article:

> When it comes to character and virtue, these young people have been left on their own. Today's go-getter parents and today's educational institutions work frantically to cultivate neural synapses, to foster good study skills, to promote musical talents. . . . We spend huge amounts of money on safety equipment and sports coaching. We sermonize about the evils of drunk driving. We expend enormous energy guiding and regulating their lives. But when it comes to character and virtue, the most mysterious area of all, suddenly the laissez-faire ethic rules: You're on your

own, Jack and Jill; go figure out what is true and just for yourselves.[2]

In this chapter we are going to examine the three different styles of parenting: *parent-centered*, *child-centered*, and *character-centered*. Parent-centered parents are more concerned with their own agenda than their child's best interests. Child-centered parents are more concerned with their child's approval than their child's well-being. Character-centered parents are more concerned with their child's character than their child's comfort. Only character-centered parents truly parent and, as a result, raise respectful children.

Let's take a closer look at each of these so you can determine if your parenting style may be inadvertently harming your child and if so, what you need to do to raise a healthy, respectful child instead.

Parent-Centered Parents

A FEW YEARS AGO, A student in my sixth-grade Sunday-school class raised her hand to share a story I've never forgotten. With tears streaming down her cheeks, she sobbed, "Miss Jill, I don't know what to do. I asked God to forgive me, but I can't forget what I saw and heard last night."

Before I could embrace her, she continued, "I thought if I asked God to forgive me, I wouldn't see the pictures anymore . . . and I'd forget the words, but they won't go away."

I moved next to her and wrapped my arms around this child as she wept uncontrollably, beyond consolation. One of her closest friends sat on the other side to hold her hand. I suggested we go to a quiet place to talk, but the little girl insisted on telling the class her story.

Saturday night she had plans to meet friends at the movies. Her dad agreed to take her, because there was a film he wanted to see playing at the same time. When they arrived at the theater, the movie she was going to see with friends was sold out. Rather than take her home, her father took her into the movie of his choice, which was a raunchy, violent film filled with everything a twelve-year-old shouldn't see or hear.

Consequently, she had not been able to sleep. She tossed and turned as the images replayed in her head all night. Why? Because her father put his own agenda before his daughter's best interests.

While this father's selfish motivation is easily seen, the motivations of many parent-centered parents are not so obvious. One mom explained it this way: "It all starts with a natural and normal desire to be a good parent. We all want to correct the mistakes we think our parents made." Another adds, "There is an element of being afraid, of not doing something that seemingly everyone else is advocating as being good for children."[3]

Still, it's not difficult to detect the motivation behind comments such as these:

+ "We'll do whatever it takes to make the team."

+ "My six-year-old is headed for Harvard."

+ "We were rejected from the only nursery school that can guarantee acceptance into the best grade school."

+ "I'm worried. My four-year-old can't read a chapter book yet. She'll never be able to compete."

All of these parents are trying to fill their own emptiness through their children's achievements. That's usually the case with parents who have an intense need for their children to be "perfect." As a result, their parenting choices are not about helping their children become all they are meant to be, but about filling the parent's own need for recognition. Parent-centered parents often persist in pushing their children to be number one in every endeavor, whether in the classroom or on the sports field. Their motto? "Nobody cares who comes in second."

With this attitude in place, pregnant women are enrolling their unborn children in *the* nursery school. Preschoolers have portfolios of artwork and videos of dance recitals to enhance their applications to elementary school. Commercial tutoring has become a $3 billion industry in the United States, partly because students who already get good grades are now expected to polish their skills even further. Scholastic Aptitude Test (SAT) tutors talk of students as young as thirteen bursting into tears because of the pressure to get into a good college.[4]

Enid Norris, a marriage and family counselor, has observed "an increasing proliferation of antidepressants for children, in part due to the increasing pressure they endure to perform, at younger and younger ages. Children are no longer allowed to be children, more symbols of their parents' prosperity and of their parents' worth."[5]

When we insist that our children become who *we* need them to be, rather than who God intends them to be, we're not parenting, we're pushing. Our efforts become about us, not our children— and our children know it. One of two things usually happens: either we push them right out of our lives, or we push them right out of living, as vividly illustrated in the memorable film *Dead Poets Society*.

In the movie, John Keating, played by Robin Williams, is an instructor at an elite boarding school for boys. He's determined to reach the hearts of his students through the education of their souls. He befriends them outside the classroom and challenges them within it. He makes them think. He makes them hungry for more knowledge.

The father of Neil Perry, one of Keating's favorite students, cares only about his son's academic accomplishments. He can't see his son; all he sees is his own image reflected in him. He views education as a necessary means for his son to become the man he needs him to be—the next great physician. But Neil has an extraordinary gift for the stage, not medicine. His classmates are awed by his talent and encourage his interest in drama.

When Neil confronts his father, his dad uses guilt to manipulate him: "I've made a great many sacrifices to have you here, Neil, and you will not let me down."

"But, you've never asked me what I want."

"You have opportunities that I never even dreamed of. I am not going to let you—"

"But I've got to tell you what I feel," Neil interrupts.

In a low, firm voice, his father replies, "If it's more of that acting business, you can forget that."

Knowing all too well that tone of voice, Neil concedes, "Yes, Sir."

His father ends the conversation with a satisfying smile and a pat on the back as he walks past his son.

"But I was good. I was really good," Neil whispers to himself as he ambles down the hallway in despair.

If you've seen the film, you know the tragic ending: a young man pushed to suicide by his parent-centered father.

> The **answers** are simple.
>
> It's parents who are difficult.
>
> —Wise Ol' Wilbur

Child-Centered Parents

CHILDREN RAISED IN CHILD-CENTERED HOMES don't fare any better than those raised in parent-centered homes. Just ask TJ.

TJ was a handsome boy who had grown up in the church. He had everything a child could hope for: parents who loved each other, nice clothes, the latest gadgets, doting grandparents, a beautiful home in a wonderful neighborhood, and enrollment in a private Christian school.

But in eighth grade, signs of trouble began surfacing: a skirmish with a classmate at school, then an incident of mouthing off to a teacher, followed by suspicion of drug use . . . all with a rapidly declining attitude at home.

When he was in ninth grade, TJ was asked not to return to his school. For the next two years he moved from one school to another. Even so, when he turned sixteen, his parents gave him a new SUV. Somehow he graduated from high school. With the freedom of college came the real trouble. TJ was out of control—lost in a world of drugs.

I talked with him a few days after I had received a distraught phone call from his mom: "He's gone again. We don't know where he is. I'm terrified we've lost him forever this time." When I asked TJ about his life and his troubles, this is what he told me:

> I just wish my parents had told me what to do. They never did. It was always whatever I wanted to do. I know they were just trying to make me happy, but I made all the decisions. I hated that . . . what does a kid do with that? When they didn't know what to do, they gave me toys. All that stuff was just garbage. They piled it on till I couldn't take it anymore.

TJ needed parents, not indulgent gift givers. So did Robert.

Robert, a second grader, came home with my sons one Friday to spend the night. Shortly after they arrived, we headed for a nearby pond to fish from the pier, as we knew this was not an everyday occurrence for Robert. After ten minutes he announced, "This is boring. What can you do with a fish if you do catch it? My dad gave me money; let's go buy something."

We stopped fishing, but we didn't go shopping; we headed home.

When I called the boys to supper, Robert came to the table with a decorated plastic container. When I asked the reason, he replied, "My mom sent it because she knows I won't eat anything else." Inside the container—a peanut butter and jelly sandwich with the edges sliced off, cut on the diagonal. I replaced his prepared plate with an empty plate. He requested a certain fruit drink that I didn't have, so he opted for no drink.

Don't get me started on Robert's bad manners, but it wasn't his fault; he had child-centered parents. Robert needed his parents to treat him as their son, rather than acting like one of his subjects. He was a classic example of what I affectionately call "aristobrats"—children treated like royalty.

> **Aristobrats:** Children treated like royalty, little Kings and Queens of the home
>
> —Wilbur's Glossary

Kids in a child-centered home are allowed to make decisions their parents should be making, the parents being more concerned with their kids' approval than their well-being. Child-centered parents often get caught in the indulgence trap: "If I just give my children enough, they will appreciate all that I've done and in return become wonderful, respectful children, because I've satisfied their desires." Unfortunately, the indulgence trap sucks you and your children in, leaving you drained and your children empty.

Regrettably, many parents seem caught in this trap. Take a look at the results from two questions in a recent poll by *Time/CNN*:

1. Are today's children more or less spoiled than children ten or fifteen years ago? Eighty percent of those who responded said *more*.

2. Are your own children spoiled or not spoiled? Sixty-

eight percent of those who responded said very/somewhat spoiled.[6]

Our materialistic society makes it difficult not to spoil children, but regardless, if children are spoiled, their parents are the only ones to blame. The media and other parents may tell us that our children *need* a cell phone by age nine or that they *need* a television in their rooms. (In 2006, 70 percent of nine-year-olds had televisions in their rooms.[7] Today, the fastest-growing age group to have televisions in their rooms is the 0-to-8 group.[8]) Ultimately, the decision of what comes into our homes is up to us. Or at least it should be.

Parents who are overworked and overtired are often tempted to fall into the trap of buying things for their kids to make up for not being there. But this never works. The overindulgence of child-centered parents offers things rather than a relationship, and this only makes matters worse. Just ask King Midas. Remember his story?

Midas was a hardworking, honest king who adored his daughter, Marigold, who loved nothing more than to spend time in the rose garden. In years past her father had shared his appreciation of the garden, teaching his daughter the complicated process of tending roses. But the more the king loved his daughter, the more he wanted to bequeath her all the gold in the world. He spent all his time thinking about how he could amass more gold rather than spending time with his daughter, all the while proclaiming it was for her that he was working so hard.

One day a stranger offered to grant King Midas one request. The king requested that everything he touched would turn to gold. The next morning King Midas arose to find his wish had come true. Everything he touched turned to gold. *What can I do for Marigold with this gift?* he thought. The king ran to the garden and transformed his daughter's beloved flowers into pure gold. Soon the entire garden sparkled in the morning sun.

King Midas returned to the palace for breakfast. He seated himself at the table and waited for his daughter to join him. Suddenly, Marigold entered the dining hall, weeping uncontrollably.

"What is the matter?" cried her father.

As she held a golden flower before him, Marigold said, "This is the ugliest flower that ever grew! I ran to the garden to gather some roses for you this morning; all the beautiful roses that smelled so sweet and were all the colors of the rainbow have turned this horrible golden-brown color."

Not able to stand her sorrow, King Midas embraced her before he realized what would happen when he touched her. "Marigold!" he cried. But Marigold could not answer. She had become a golden statue, the victim of her father's desire for wealth.

Unlike what happens in real life, this children's tale ends well. The stranger returned and told Midas how he could rid himself of the "golden touch." Midas followed the instructions and restored his daughter and her garden to their fragile beauty. The only gold that King Midas ever desired to see again was the golden strands of his daughter's hair.

Like King Midas, indulgent parents fool themselves into believing their obsession with things is for the good of their children. But providing for your kids is much more than providing them with the latest electronic devices, name-brand clothes, and a car at sixteen. Children don't want *things* from their parents. They don't need the gold; they need you.

Keep in mind that overindulgence isn't just buying toys and things; it's also doing for kids what they should be doing for themselves.

Case in point: A one-sided "conversation" with an exasperated friend went something like this: "I don't know what I'm going to do with Maggie. I can't take her anymore, and I don't understand why she's the way she is." Without taking a breath, my friend continued, "I've done everything for this child. She's never had to do anything around here. I don't feel like I expect too much. Last night when I asked her to put her wet towels in the laundry basket, not on the carpet, you would have thought I asked her to scrub the toilet! But the new problem is homework. She's decided it's too hard and doesn't want to try. She's in middle school . . . I can't do her homework for her anymore."

Can't do her homework for her *anymore?*

Kids need parents who will teach them age-appropriate life skills, whether it is tying their shoes, cleaning their rooms, or doing their homework. They need parents who will teach and watch and wait, parents who have the patience to allow their children to struggle enough to learn a new skill.

The more we give our kids, the less they appreciate *us*, which leads to disrespect. To respect means to hold in high regard. We can't respect someone we do not appreciate. This was brought home to me several years ago when my sons were in elementary school. I found myself fussing at them for not being appreciative, after I had foolishly indulged them. One of the boys stopped me in my tracks: "Mom, when I grow up . . . I think my kids will love me more if I give them less."

When we give too much and expect too little, we end up with kids who are selfish and unappreciative. We're not training them to be independent; we're training them to be dependent on us. If we're not equipping them with the tools they need to stand on their own two feet, they'll soon need a crutch. What they choose to lean on varies greatly from one child to the next. TJ, a "good boy" from a "good home," found his crutch through a dependency on drugs. His rebellion against his parents was a loud, long "Stop, I can't take anymore!" Indulgence produces resentment, which leads to rebellion.

> **Indulgence** produces resentment, which leads to rebellion.
> —Wise Ol' Wilbur

Neither the parent-centered parent nor the child-centered

parent gives children what they need; they have, in fact, relinquished their responsibility to parent well. When parents carefully take on their parenting responsibility and focus on producing character in their children, their children flourish. Let's explore what's different about this third parenting style.

Character-Centered Parents

MIKE AND LISA CONN ARE two of the most character-centered parents I know. The effectiveness of this parenting style can be seen in the lives of their three children.

Ali and her older sister, Ashley, both graduated from high school with top honors, earning scholarships to a great university. They didn't drink or smoke, and they didn't date boys who did.

Ali took a dream trip as a college sophomore—six weeks in Europe. In order to afford the trip, she worked summers, vacations, and every chance in between from the time she entered high school. Her parents helped with a small gift, but Ali paid her own way.

Both girls were popular, even though they were different from

> Many well-bred people *neglect* laying down any rules for the guidance of their children. . . . Parents owe it to their children and to society to instruct them how to be gentle, courteous, and above all, self-denying. Teach them to respect each other's rights, to enjoy their merry romp and innocent fun without hurting each other's feelings, or playing upon some weakness.
>
> —Youth's Educator for Home and Society (1896)

their peers. Their closets weren't filled with seldom-worn clothes. They didn't own expensive sports cars or the latest gadgets. Still, they never complained—quite the contrary.

These girls had goals and a work ethic to reach those goals. They didn't have to be entertained to be content. They commanded respect without trying, because they were always ready to help a friend, regardless of inconvenience.

I've never witnessed girls who love their father the way these girls do. They not only love him, but they also respect his word. And their mother? She's best friend to both.

And Aimee, who's still at home? She's following in her older sisters' footsteps—destined to become another daughter who returns blessings to her parents tenfold. She is a self-disciplined fourteen-year-old, who just earned a first-degree black belt in Taekwondo from the American Martial Arts Institute. With six-day-a-week workouts, she uses her free time at school to fill in the study gaps, maintaining a grade point average that rivals her sisters'.

I was privileged to attend the weddings of both Ashley and Ali to fine young men. Ashley is now the proud mother of two little ones. She often calls home for advice from the parenting experts she trusts the most. Ali continues to use her extraordinary art talent to bless others.

What do character-centered parents do that is so different from parent-centered and child-centered parents? They have their priorities in the proper order. See if you don't agree.

1. *Character-centered parents parent with the end in mind.* They make decisions that are focused on the desired end result—children who respect God, others, and themselves. Stephen Covey, author of *The 7 Habits of Highly Effective People*, explains this concept well:

   > The *end* represents the *purpose* of your life. Until
   > you can say what that purpose is, with assurance,

then you just cannot direct your life in the manner that would bring you the greatest satisfaction. There are no shortcuts here. To engage in this habit, you need to have a dream, define your own vision, and get into the practice of setting goals which will allow you to make measurable progress toward the dream . . . to re-align your efforts so that you will ultimately achieve your heart's desire.[9]

Character-centered parents accept the dream and challenge of raising respectful children, and they define that vision by choosing to focus on building their children's character above all other endeavors. It's about who their children are becoming. Parenting with the end in mind is intentional, not accidental.

Mike and Lisa have done a beautiful job of establishing their home with the end in mind. Their girls have proven it.

2. *Character-centered parents look to God's principles for their instructions on how to parent.* They know they can't trust their own wits to raise their children, nor can they trust the "child experts," since these "experts" are responsible for the misguided advice that got us into trouble in the first place. So they rely on the wisdom that comes from biblical teaching, not the knowledge from psychology books. (Our society has changed parenting approaches numerous times in the past two hundred years, but the Bible has remained unchanged for two thousand years.)

3. *Character-centered parents keep their promises.* I'm convinced that Matthew, the author of the first book in the New Testament, was talking to parents when he said, "Do not swear by your head, for you cannot make even one hair white or

black. [Your children will do this for you.] Simply let your 'Yes' be 'Yes,' and your 'No,' 'No.'"[10] If our children trust us, they will obey us. This, in turn, leads them to respect us and, ultimately, God.

Keep in mind that kids make no distinction between a semi-affirmative answer and a promise. In other words:

✦ You say, "We'll see."

> Child hears: "It'll probably be okay. Sure."

> You meant: "Probably no, but I'll take another look at it."

✦ You say, "Honey, I'll have to think about it."

> Child hears: "Keep asking me; I'll probably give in."

> You meant: "I can't decide now; I'm uncomfortable with the idea, but I need a good reason to say no."

Children cannot distinguish the gray in our answers because their world is black and white, right or wrong, as it should be. If you mean no, say, "No."

4. *Character-centered parents put God first, then their marriage, children, others, and finally themselves.* We all have our priorities, whether we're conscious of them or not. The decisions you make reveal your priorities. The consequences of your decisions bring either the devastation or preservation of your family.

The Character-Centered Parents' Priority List

God

Husband/Wife

Children

Others

Self

Most of us want to put ourselves first (narcissistic tendency), but to do so guarantees disaster for our kids. Selfishness is at the root of our most devastating parenting decisions. Take a moment to reflect back on the parent-centered dad who stole his daughter's innocence by taking her to that R-rated movie. This father put *himself* on top of the list rather than God, who would not have exposed a twelve-year-old to an R-rated movie. A character-centered dad would have taken his daughter home with the promise that he'd take her to see the children's movie she wanted to see another time.

Why do character-centered parents put their marriage before their kids? Because children need to know their parents' love for each other is the foundation of their love for them. Kids who know this grow up feeling secure. When a parent claims to no longer love the other parent, the children lose the foundation of the parents' love for them. That's why divorce is so destructive for children. Character-centered parents keep the marriage ahead of the children, others, and, above all, ahead of self!

Character-centered parents don't put other people's needs ahead of their children's. They understand that even good activities can be wrong if children suffer as a result of Mom or Dad's involvement. If supper comes from McDonald's three nights a week because of Mom's meetings, her priority list has gotten out of order. "Others" have moved above the children.

The list of priorities shown here must not be rearranged, or the family will suffer. When *God* is the head of the home and you honor each other as *husband and wife*, the rest of the priority list will stay in intact.

+ You will be able to work together to train your *children*.

+ You can reach out to *others* as a family.

+ God will take care of each of you, for God honors the family that honors Him.

Your Child's Heart

A WOUNDED TWENTY-YEAR-OLD SUMMARIZED THE pitfalls of parent-centered and child-centered parenting better than I ever could. When asked what makes teenagers more miserable today than in past generations, she gave the following reply:

Teenagers don't know who they are. They don't know what to believe in because their parents say one thing, but live another. You know, most parents today don't have good answers; they just put you off when you ask the big questions because they're still trying to figure out what's really important.

Parents think their kids really want a lot of stuff. Maybe we do, but it's just a substitute for the real thing. Teenagers have to know they're number one with somebody. Most of the time my parents were so caught up in their own world, they didn't see how much I needed them. I wanted to be more important to Dad than his work. I wanted to be more important to Mom than her church friends. It's not so much time as it is a heart thing. You know if it's there, and you know if it's not there. If you don't feel it from your parents, you're going to keep looking till you find it somewhere.

She nailed the truth, didn't she?

When I speak, I often draw the outline of a heart on a chalk-board as I pose the following question to my audience: "Today you have the opportunity to fill the empty heart of a child. What will you place in that heart?"

Regardless of the makeup of the audience, the answers are the same. We seem to agree, regardless of faith, socioeconomic standing, or race, that children need the following qualities:

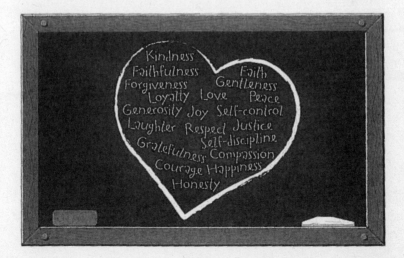

Did you notice that *respect* is at the center of the heart? Just as it should be.

Now, take a long, hard look at the drawing. Why don't we see more young people filled with these attitudes and attributes? I believe it's because too many parents don't parent. They neglect the education of their children's hearts.

If you choose to be a character-centered parent, you can fill your children's hearts with all they need to become all they were created to be. Helen Keller's words remind us, "Character cannot be developed in ease and quiet. Only through experience of trial and suffering can the soul be strengthened, vision cleared, ambition inspired, and success achieved."[11]

I'm not going to tell you it's easy, because it's not. But I am going to tell you that it can be done.

3

Enroll in the School of Respect

ANYONE LIVING ON or near the Gulf Coast understands the critical need to be prepared for natural disasters, because good preparation can minimize the damage. Boarding up windows, gathering survival supplies, and even taking a class on storm readiness, which includes developing a "family survival plan," are essential parts of preparedness. The better prepared you are for a storm, the greater your chance of survival.

As Hurricane Isaac approached, there was little excuse for not being aware of the dangers ahead and the preparation needed. We had been through this drill many times in the past. Days before the storm hit, hardware store shelves began emptying of basic supplies, including candles, matches, and batteries. Grocery shelves were restocked with water and canned goods as fast as they were cleared. This time around, the warnings were heeded and preparations were made, even though no one could predict where the storm would make landfall.

It's one thing to be prepared for the dangers that might come from a storm you're watching on the Weather Channel; it's quite another to be prepared for the inevitable dangers your children will face in the storms that rage out of control in our disrespectful world. How can you be adequately prepared to face the onslaught of squalls from your two-year-old? How can you stand your ground when your ten-year-old wants to watch an R-rated movie at his friend's house? How can you go against the flow when your teenager asks to attend *the* party where "everybody" is going, when you know adults will not be present?

In this chapter, you'll be invited to enroll in a "storm readiness" school that walks you through the four stages of child development, helping you create a family survival plan. At each stage, there are "soul" questions that need to be settled to prepare your children for the next level of maturity. No matter the ages of your children, you will be able to identify struggles they are experiencing based on a soul question that has not yet been answered. (Many have written to say "The School of Respect" chart is the most helpful piece of information in the book.)

Knowing the soul questions that need to be answered and the most effective training method to answer those questions, you will be well equipped to guide your children through the turbulent stages of growing up from tots to teens.

You'll never have all the answers for every storm surge, but if you stick to your plan, you won't be caught unprepared—as I was the day Boyce brought home a less-than-exemplary report card.

* * *

MY TEN-YEAR-OLD SON, BOYCE, FOLDED his report card in half as he held it before my eyes. "Look, Mom, I made all A's."

"Yes, you did!" I agreed. But when I unfolded the card to look at the right side, my glowing quickly turned to gloom. All but one of those little squares on the right were filled with ugly U's and even a

U-minus rather than beautiful S's. His card looked something like this:

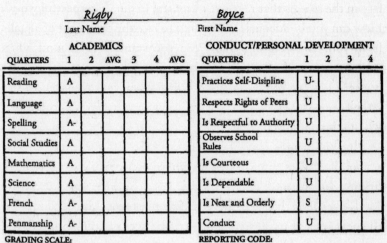

Rigby						Boyce				
Last Name						First Name				

ACADEMICS						CONDUCT/PERSONAL DEVELOPMENT				
QUARTERS	1	2	AVG	3	4	AVG	QUARTERS	1	2	3	4

ACADEMICS QUARTERS	1	2	AVG	3	4	AVG
Reading	A					
Language	A					
Spelling	A-					
Social Studies	A					
Mathematics	A					
Science	A					
French	A-					
Penmanship	A-					

CONDUCT/PERSONAL DEVELOPMENT QUARTERS	1	2	3	4
Practices Self-Disipline	U-			
Respects Rights of Peers	U			
Is Respectful to Authority	U			
Observes School Rules	U			
Is Courteous	U			
Is Dependable	U			
Is Neat and Orderly	S			
Conduct	U			

GRADING SCALE:
A=100–94 B=93–86 C=85-77 D=76-70 F=69-Below

REPORTING CODE:
S=Satisfactory N=Needs Improvement U=Unsatisfactory

When I flipped the card over, I found his teacher's comments: "Report card is wonderful . . . however, I want that conduct to improve. He says things without thinking. Sometimes his words hurt other people's feelings." Needless to say, Mrs. Manners was devastated.

The wise words of an educator I'd heard speak years before rang in my ears: "You can make all A's and still flunk the school of life." If I didn't do something drastic, my son would flunk the school of life. Neither of my sons was going to learn respect or manners at school alone. They needed to learn these lessons first at home. I decided right then to enroll them in the School of Respect.

The best way to raise respectful kids is to enroll them in the School of Respect as soon as they are born. Babies come into this world with a need to be taught and trained. Their first understanding of respect comes from their interaction with their parents, even in the first months of life. Even if unspoken, they have questions that must be answered, and they naturally look to their parents for those answers.

The book of Proverbs instructs parents: "Train a child in the way he should go."[1] The original Hebrew word for "train" is *chanak*, which means "to initiate or discipline or dedicate."[2] "Way," or *derek*, means "a course of life or mode of action."[3] So the original intent of this passage is: "Discipline a child for his course of life and the actions he should take."

Noah Webster understood this verse's true meaning. Peek into the pages of *Webster's* 1828 edition with me to find an excellent definition for *education*:

> The bringing up of a child with instruction . . . formation of manners. Education comprehends all that series of instruction and discipline which is intended to enlighten the understanding, correct the temper, and form the manners and habits of youth, and fit them for usefulness in their future stations.[4]

Parents who enroll their children in the School of Respect are undergirding their children's formal education, because respect lies at the foundation of success. In an interesting study a few years ago, Alberta Siegel, a noted researcher at Stanford University, concluded:

> When it comes to rearing children, every society is only twenty years away from barbarism. Twenty years is all we have to accomplish the task of civilizing the infants who are born into our midst each year. These savages know nothing of our language, our culture, our religion, our values, our customs of interpersonal relations. The infant is totally ignorant about . . . respect, decency, honesty, customs, conventions, and manners.[5]

A bit harsh, perhaps, but a point well taken. God has given us twenty years to educate our children's hearts and to train them to respect Him, others, and self so that they can become respectful members of society who help, rather than hurt, the world.

The School of Respect

THE SCHOOL OF RESPECT HAS four distinct stages, according to age: *Tots* (birth to age two), *Tykes* (ages three to five), *Tweens* (ages six to twelve), and *Teens* (ages thirteen to nineteen). Each stage has a different developmental goal, and parents need to utilize specific training methods to help their children meet each of those goals. During each stage, children have two critical soul questions, which parents need to answer. Parents who successfully answer these two questions give their kids a vital part of the preparation they need to become respectful, responsible young adults.

Why are these questions called "soul" questions? Because they get to the heart of the matter. We can't expect our two-year-old to trust what we say unless she is sure we are in charge. We can't expect our five-year-old to step into kindergarten with enough confidence to cross the threshold of the classroom unless he knows whom he belongs to and that his parent is watching out for him.

An elementary school principal asked to be excused from a meeting in her office after hearing a child cry for several minutes. She returned shortly with a precious little boy who had obviously been upset. How unusual to see a child stop crying when entering the principal's office!

He cried every morning when his mom left. The only comfort he found was in the principal's office. The principal made the comment that he was afraid. She had assured the little boy's mom that he would get over it with time. I couldn't help but ask if anyone had asked the child what he was afraid of. With a small grin on the principal's face, the answer was "no."

When the little boy was finally asked what he was afraid of, he answered, "This isn't my house." This sweet child didn't have the security of knowing someone from home was watching out for him even though he was away. He needed answers to the soul questions: "Are you watching me?" and "Who do I belong to?" We suggested taking a photo of his mom and turning it into a button he could carry in his pocket.

I'm so pleased to say it worked better than a charm.

THE SCHOOL OF RESPECT		
Stage	**Goal**	**Training**
Tots: Birth to two	Trust	Routine
Tykes: Three to five	Security	Recognition
Tweens: Six to twelve	Obedience	Relationship
Teens: Thirteen to nineteen	Self-Respect	Responsibility

Let's take a closer look at each of these four stages and the complementary soul questions.

Stage 1: Building Trust in Tots through Routine

BABIES COME INTO THE WORLD totally dependent on their parents to meet their every need—physical, mental, social, and emotional. We meet our babies' physical needs by feeding, bathing, and clothing them; their mental needs by providing a stimulating environment; and their social needs through providing safe interaction with others. We meet their emotional needs by answering two key questions.

QUESTION 1: Can I trust you?

DURING THIS STAGE YOUR TOT is striving to learn trust, which is his first developmental goal. What training method will help you answer this question for your child? *Routine*. If you provide a routine for your tot, you will be answering this critical question with a resounding yes. Your tot learns to trust you when you put him on a schedule for feeding and sleeping.

I realize that feeding and sleeping schedules are sometimes criticized as being parent-centered, but look at it from your baby's perspective. If he knows that he will be fed and put to bed at the same time every day, your baby doesn't have to become distressed before someone feeds him or cranky before someone puts him down for a nap. He learns he can trust you to meet his needs, and he can relax in his environment.

My own experience has convinced me that this is so. When our twin sons were born, I was fortunate to have an old-fashioned pediatrician who stressed the importance of scheduled feedings; and with his help, I had the boys on a four-hour feeding schedule six weeks after they were born.

Outings were a treat for all of us because the boys were content; they knew their needs would be met. Each day we followed a routine, and this made their lives secure and our lives serene. (Well, most days—don't think there weren't difficult days.)

The day began with breakfast, a nap, then playtime. After they ate lunch, I put them down for an extended nap, then took them on an afternoon stroll. When we arrived back home, they had more playtime. The day closed with supper, baths (which became playtime when they were toddlers), downtime, and bedtime. As much as possible, we did these things at the same time every day.

When we provide routines for our kids and follow those routines day by day, we are slowly answering the first critical question of this stage in the School of Respect. Through our routines we are showing our children that, yes, they can trust us to take care of their needs—and we are helping them take their first step toward respecting authority.

Parents also build trust by answering this next question.

QUESTION 2: Who's in charge?

AS I MENTIONED EARLIER, I'VE often wondered if when Jesus spoke the words (in Matthew 5:36–37) "Let your 'Yes' be 'Yes,' and your 'No,' 'No,'" He was thinking of parents—more specifically, parents of a toddler. Tots want to know who's in charge (and they are hoping you are, because they know they don't have a clue what to do). That's why they say the word *no* so often. They want to know if you are in charge and will tell them what they have to do.

This is why I disagree with the notion of removing knick-knacks from tabletops when couples start having kids. Accessories provide parents opportunities to teach their kids that the parent—not the child—is in charge, that the parents' "no" overrides the children's "no." If you'll patiently take on this battle at home, your child will be welcome in anyone's home, because she'll know not to touch.

Establishing that you are in charge will go a long way toward making bedtime a more enjoyable experience when your tot turns two. Bedtime is one of the early testing grounds of your authority. If you have already demonstrated that your "no" means no, your child will be less likely to wage a major battle with you every night when you try to put her to bed.

Your tot's bedtime routine aids in answering this "Who's in charge?" question. Every night when you put her to bed, read her a bedtime story, snuggle, give plenty of good-night kisses and hugs, and pray with her as you tuck her in, safe and sound. No exceptions. Such a routine will make it far less likely that she will get up fifteen times during the night or end up sleeping in the hallway outside your door.

If we could decode what our tots mean when they are wailing, we might hear, "Daddy, I'm going to see if you *really* mean what you say" or "Mommy, I'm going to scream, just to see if you really love me." This is why I cannot stress strongly enough the importance of establishing routines during the first two years of your children's lives. Routines build trust, and if your children trust you as infants, they'll feel more secure as tykes.

Stage 2: Developing Security in Tykes through Recognition

JUSTIN STOOD ON TOP OF the giant slide at Bayberry Park as a confident five-year-old superhero preparing for a death-defying feat. Scanning the area, he spotted his heroine, who was engaged in a deep conversation with a friend.

"Moooooommmm!" he shouted. No response.

He tried again, "Mom, Mom, Mooooooooooooommmmm . . . watch this!"

"Okay, honey, I'm watching!" Mom yelled back, continuing her conversation.

Still not satisfied, he tried one more time: "Mom, you're not watching!"

"Honey, I'm watching, I'm watching!" she fired back in exasperation.

Justin finally made the big leap down the slide, hoping Mom was watching. When he reached the bottom, he looked at Mom, who wasn't watching. Instead of running to her, he ran from her.

Please . . . don't make the mistake of this mom.

In this second stage, kids discover the world—people, places, and things. They don't want to miss any of it, but they need a sense of security to be able to engage with their exciting new world.

How do we help our tykes develop a sense of security? Through the training method of *recognition*. Parents can use recognition to answer the two key questions of this stage.

QUESTION 1: Are you watching me?

BETWEEN THE AGES OF THREE and five, your tyke needs to know you're watching him. If he discovers you are watching, his trust in you will grow. But if he discovers you are not watching him, whatever trust has been established up to this point will erode. He needs to know that you will be there to protect him if he needs protection. If you watch him now, in time, he will stop asking you to watch him because he will have developed the security he needs to explore the world unafraid.

When one of my sons was four, he managed to escape the watchful eyes of his parents and grandparents and wander through the halls of the American Museum of Natural History in New York. We found him clinging to a handrail, mesmerized by a display of prehistoric creatures. When I knelt down beside him, he looked at me with tear-filled eyes of gratitude, and said, "I'm okay, Mom; I wasn't scared. I knew you would find me." At that moment, I knew my son felt secure . . . maybe a little bit too secure!

When children know we are watching out for them, they feel protected. This frees them to be more giving to others. For instance, a four-year-old who knows her parents are there for her has the security to be unselfish, to share with her playmates, and to help them. She has the freedom to show concern for others because she's not consumed with watching out for herself—a beautiful by-product of security.

Recognition also helps you answer the second question of this stage.

QUESTION 2: Who do I belong to?

POINTING TO HER CHEST, FOUR-YEAR-OLD Rebecca asked her mom, "Who am I?"

"You're Rebecca. Rebecca Thompson."

"Not my name. Who am I on the inside?" Rebecca questioned.

Her mom answered, "You're God's child. He placed you in our family to be loved and cared for."

When her daughter asked, "Who am I?" Rebecca's mom seized a teachable moment, an opportunity to recognize who her daughter was, thus giving her security. She went on to tell her daughter about the day she was born, as well as other anecdotes from her days as an infant.

This wise mom was answering her daughter's real question: *Whom do I belong to?* Children have a deep need to belong, to fit in. They need to be recognized as part of the family circle, and when they are recognized as such, they develop security.

Because children this age need to be accepted—to belong— they're eager to please. Hasn't your young child ever asked, "Can I help?" I know it's easier to unload the dishwasher yourself than to allow a four-year-old to help, but when you let your child help with chores, you are giving her an opportunity to feel a part of the family. Kids this age can do simple household chores, such as helping with dinner, hanging up clothes, putting wet towels in the laundry basket, and picking up their toys. When they accomplish such tasks, they begin to feel a sense of value and worth. They begin to think:

+ "My family needs me to do my part."

+ "They can't make it without me."

+ I want to help my family as much as they help me."

When children know they're valued members of the family, it gives them a deep sense of security. When they reach adolescence, this security creates a firm foundation for them to stand on as they branch out from the family during the tumultuous tween years.

Stage 3: Helping Tweens Learn Obedience through Relationship

CHILDREN WHO HAVE DEVELOPED TRUST in their early years and gained a sense of security in their tyke years are in a position to master the developmental goal of the tween years: *obedience*. Obedience, which is critical at this stage when children are extending beyond the boundaries of the family, is a learned response. We aren't born with a natural inclination to obey. Quite the contrary, we're born with an inclination to disobey.

What, then, causes children to obey their parents? What training method will help your children learn obedience? Your *relationship* with them. During this stage your children want to know if you really love them, and they will test you on this question, over and over again.

QUESTION 1: Do you really love me?

TWEENS DESPERATELY NEED TO BE loved. This is an extension of needing to belong. You must be the one to satisfy the need behind this question, because kids obey the person who loves them. If your tween doesn't know you love him, he will search in the wrong places for someone who does.

Keep in mind that a tween's disobedience is often a test of your love. A ten-year-old is most likely not going to ask in words, "Do you really love me?" Instead, he asks through his actions. How can you let your children know you *really* love them during the tween years, cultivating obedience rather than disobedience? By:

1. *Listening to your tweens.* Think of the E. F. Hutton commercial—when your children talk, you'd better listen. Just as your three-year-old needed you to watch him, your nine-year-old needs you to listen when she speaks to you. And I don't mean the "uh-huh" kind of listening. Listen to your tweens with all your being. Listen with your eyes. Listen with your ears. Listen with your heart. When you're too tired to listen, listen anyway. If you will listen to tweens when they're nine, they'll obey you when they're sixteen.

2. *Telling your tweens "no" when "no" is better than "yes."* Scripture teaches that discipline shows children they are loved. When you love enough to say "no," you are showing your kids you care about who they are and who they will become.

   Here are some ways to discipline with love:

   ✦ *Speak in a firm voice without sarcasm.* Sarcasm conveys disgust, not love. Use of sarcasm teaches your child to use the same tone with you in the teen years.

   ✦ *Say to your child, "I love you too much to allow you to* (go to the late show with friends, go to a party without parents present, or be disrespectful of your sister)."

   ✦ *Don't berate your child, but correct the misdeed.* You know those words that still haunt you from your childhood, "Why aren't you smart enough to listen?" and "I don't care what you think." Instead, say, "I know you're smart, so I know you can choose to listen. When you choose to listen, we'll talk." "I hear your viewpoint, but I will not allow you to spend the night at your friend's house without my calling her mom or dad. It's your choice."

✦ *Don't lose your temper.* Instead, count—to five hundred if necessary. Don't laugh . . . I started counting one afternoon when I lost my patience with my sons during a long car ride. When I reached one hundred, the boys asked how high I was going to count. When I said to five hundred, they promised to settle down if I would just stop counting!

✦ *Turn a negative situation into a positive one.* Remind your child that she is too smart or too talented or too old to act in an inappropriate way. Acknowledge your tween's value, and she'll live up to your expectations. When your tween forgets to do her chores, say, "I'm counting on you to do your chores, because I know you're old enough to handle the responsibility."

Your tweens will be assured of your love when you listen to their ramblings. They will accept your discipline when it comes from your heart.

Not only do tweens need to know their parents love them, they also need to know their parents are real.

QUESTION 2: Are you real?

JUST AS TWEENS WILL OBEY the person who truly loves them, they'll obey the person they can look up to. If we expect obedience from our tweens, we must be authentic persons our children can trust above all others.

Your tween daughter is growing up in a time when there are few worthy role models. In fact, very few people in your tween's world are real—they're not who they're pretending to be. Musicians are lip-synching, fashion models are airbrushed, and sports stars are cheating. Your tween is looking for authenticity in someone—and that someone needs to be you.

Keep in mind that children learn more from what we do than from what we say. This is particularly true during the tween years, when we parents can no longer fool our kids. (Not that we really ever could.)

They're watching our every move and seeing if our actions match our words. An Old Testament passage gives parents instruction in this area: "Be careful, and watch yourselves closely so that you do not forget the things your eyes have seen or let them slip from your heart as long as you live. Teach them to your children and to their children after them."[6]

If you're not authentic, your children will rebel in disrespect toward you and, often, toward society. Children respect parents who are respectable. If you expect from yourself that which you expect from your children, you'll all pass this test. Be the person you want your child to become. We teach what we know, but we reproduce who we are.

What should your authenticity look like to your tween?

1. *Be the same on the inside as you appear on the outside.* In other words, you can't be one person out in the world and another person behind the doors of your home.

2. *Don't say one thing and do another.* Drinking one too many on Saturday nights disqualifies you in the eyes of your tween to discuss the hazards of drinking.

3. *Be honest in your business dealings.* Children in this age bracket listen and watch you more intently than your

supervisor at work. They need you to be the most honest person they know.

4. Don't show any hypocrisy. This will lose your tween's respect faster than any other weakness. Do you enter church when the doors open, but never open the Bible for study? Do you pray in public, but not with your family?

Your tweens are more likely to obey when you meet their need for love and authenticity. If your tween is being disobedient, revisit these two questions and check your heart to see if you've given your child satisfying answers. It could be that you've let your guard down in an area. It's not too late; kids are more than willing to give parents another chance. They want us to succeed in raising them to be respectful. They need us to succeed.

A tween who turns thirteen with an obedient heart is ready for the final stage in the parenting process, the development of self-respect.

Stage 4: Teaching Self-Respect through Responsibility

TEENS ARE SEARCHING—FOR TRUTH, for answers to life, and for themselves. During this final stage, the disrespectful world can thwart you in your goal of raising a respectful teenager.

Your challenge is to help your teenager develop self-respect, because in so doing, his questions will be answered and his search will end in success. Teens with healthy self-respect discover that the secret to finding themselves is to find satisfaction in making wise choices and in offering respect to others.

If you want to help your teenagers develop self-respect, you must instill the understanding that:

✦ The reasons we do what we do are more important than what we do.

✦ We were put here to serve, not to be served.

✦ What we give is more important than what we are given.

✦ Through humility we gain confidence.

What's the training method that can help you teach your teen self-respect? *Responsibility*. During this stage, you need to begin moving the responsibility for your teen's development from your shoulders to his. The more responsibility you give your teen, the more opportunities he'll have for success and the building of self-respect. With each accomplishment, your teen's self-respect grows. George Bernard Shaw understood this principle of building self-respect when he said, "No man who is occupied in doing a very difficult thing, and doing it very well, ever loses his self-respect."[7] Teens with self-respect know there are consequences for their choices and are ready to accept the challenge of being in charge.

Let's look at the first question we need to help our teens answer.

QUESTION 1: Who am I?

MORE THAN ELEVEN THOUSAND TEENAGERS, ages twelve to seventeen, were surveyed as part of the National Longitudinal Study of Adolescent Health to determine which factors were most helpful in preventing risky behavior, such as substance abuse, early sexual involvement, teen pregnancy, violence, and suicide.[8] The findings reinforced a fundamental belief of character-centered parents: teenagers who have the presence of a parent before school, after school, at dinnertime, and at bedtime are less likely to engage in risky behaviors than those without parental connectedness.

In a radio interview about the study, lead researcher Dr. Michael Resnick commented:

> I think that fundamentally what the study did is to challenge a widespread myth that we have in the United States, which is that once a child has moved from early childhood into adolescence, what parents say or think or do or hope or dream for their child, somehow no longer makes a difference. And many parents in this country . . . feel that once a kid has reached adolescence, they must surrender that child to the peer group—and in fact that is not the case. We found that across the board in aggregate for our kids that sense of closeness and caring with parents, including for older adolescents, was a very important determinant of health and well being.[9]

Larry Crabb calls this "connecting"[10] and says that parents must make a heart connection to enable their children to find themselves. Your teen's greatest hope of answering the question "Who am I?" comes from her connection with you. Her teen years are the time in her life when she must know there's nothing she can do to make you love her more and nothing she can do to make you love her less. Your unconditional love and faith in her enables her to become confident in knowing herself.

I know the attitudes you see in teens may lead you to believe that your teen doesn't need you anymore, but it's just the opposite. Your teen needs your presence now more than ever. Teens have so much to discover about themselves, and you need to be the one to guide your teen and be there for him when he makes mistakes. Your goal is to enable your teen to face the world with enough self-respect to thrive in it!

Help your child answer the question of who he is by emphasizing that the choices we make determine who we become. For example:

1. *Allow your child to experience the consequences of poor choices.* For example, rather than insisting your sixteen-year-old go to bed at 10:00 on Friday night before a big Saturday-morning soccer game, allow him to choose his own bedtime. When he lets his team down because he's too tired to play his best, he'll learn how to set priorities.

2. *Allow mistakes to mold character.* For example, let's say your seventeen-year-old son decided to mud ride with friends on private property. You find out about it, and you know he destroyed the grass that was just beginning to sprout. Talk with him about this, and require that he apologize to the neighbor and make restitution. Go with him to apologize to the owners of the property and to inform them that he will pay for the damaged sod to be replaced and do the work to replace it. (You will need to work with your teen on how he will come up with the funds for this, of course!)

3. *Ask thought-provoking questions.* These can help you transfer the responsibility for your teen's maturing to him.

   + What do you believe about premarital sex? (Teens know your opinion, but have you asked theirs?)

   + What are your goals for yourself . . . I know what your dad and I would like to see you accomplish, but what do *you* want to accomplish?

   + What's more important to you, character or money?

   + How's your relationship with God? (The journey of self-discovery for your teen begins with you and ends with God. Ultimately, your teen must decide for herself if she will receive God's recon-

ciliation through Jesus Christ. You can show the
way by your own walk of faith.)

This list could go on forever. See that this kind of dialogue between you and your child never stops. As your relationship role
shifts from authority figure to friend, these conversations can continue to deepen.

I can't overemphasize the need to stay connected to your teens.
You must be available to listen when they need to talk to you, not
just when you need to talk to them. Talking is easy; listening is hard.
If you wait until teens ask you for your opinion, they're more likely
to hear your answer. During this time of their self-discovery, your
opinions can have a greater impact on their self-image and the
building of their self-respect than our society wants you to believe.

Now let's look at the second question of this stage.

QUESTION 2: Can I be in charge?

OUR CULTURE NO LONGER OFFERS absolute truth. Instead, it says
that whatever feels good is good and right. While *we* may know that
just because something feels good doesn't mean it's right, ultimately
our kids need to learn this lesson for themselves.

It's hard for parents to give teenagers responsibility for dealing
with their own problems, because often the consequences of their
behavior might be embarrassing or uncomfortable. But this is another great gift you can give your teen—the gift of growing up. As
Henry Ward Beecher once said, "You cannot teach a child to take
care of himself unless you will let him take care of himself."[11] So give
your teen more responsibility; just be careful not to give too much
too soon. Giving a teen too much responsibility too fast is as dangerous as giving a two-year-old a butcher knife and saying, "Now, don't
cut yourself." When parents give teens too much responsibility, they

set them up to fail and perhaps to put themselves in danger. So give teens appropriate responsibility, and give it one step at a time.

Here are some ideas for how you can help your teen succeed at being in charge of his life:

1. *Put teens in charge of developing their own talents.* Up until now you have controlled the practice schedule; now it's time to relinquish that control so your teen reaps the rewards of a job well done, as he develops the self-discipline to practice.

2. *If you haven't given cooking lessons yet, this is the time to start.* Build your teen's confidence in the kitchen by having him prepare supper one night a week. (Teens need to learn this life skill before they leave home.)

3. *Ask your teen's opinion on current events.* Engage in conversations about politics. Discuss the candidates and the issues during election season. Prepare your teen for the day she will cast a ballot.

4. *Encourage decision-making.* Rather than telling your fifteen-year-old that it's time to do homework, remind him that the rule of the house is no television before homework is completed. Let him make the decision as to when he'll do his homework. Enforce the rule, but let him choose to skip his favorite TV show because he chose not to do his homework before the program started.

5. *When mistakes are made, don't rescue your teen; instead, help your child resolve the problem.* Discuss options to rectify a mistake. She'll never be able to take charge of her own life until she learns to resolve conflicts and solve problems on her own.

6. *Help teens develop goals and determine a method to accomplish those goals, and then step back and watch.* Set aside a Saturday at the beginning of ninth grade to discuss your child's goals for high school. Write down the goals regarding such things as grade point average, class emphasis, extracurricular activities, and church and community involvement. Assess how much time it will take to participate in each activity. Point out that to do one thing well is much better than to just participate in several things. Encourage your teen to use the goal sheet as a guide for decision-making.

7. *Wait to be asked your opinion.* Don't offer unsolicited advice, unless there's danger.

8. *Remind your teens that God is in charge of us all.* I did this by having my sons read a few verses from the book of Proverbs every day before they left for high school. Yes, it was hard to do this every day, but the practical words found in God's Word helped to guide the boys' thinking during the day.

Graduation from the School of Respect

YOUR CHILD'S TEEN YEARS ARE the culmination of all you've worked hard to accomplish until now. If there's trouble in the teen years, the breakdown probably started years earlier. Disrespectfulness comes from disappointment—not because a teen didn't get the things he wanted, but because he didn't get the things he needed to fill his heart with wisdom and respect.

Our children need us to have strong relationships with them, and they need us to be role models they can trust. If we understand the questions our children are asking, we can give them the guidance they need to enter the world.

THE SCHOOL OF RESPECT		
Stage	**Goal**	**Training**
Tots: *Birth to two* Can I trust you? Who's in charge?	Trust	Establish Routines Set a schedule Be the parent
Tykes: *Three to five* Are you watching me? Who do I belong to?	Security	Offer Recognition Pay attention Show ownership
Tweens: *Six to twelve* Do you really love me? Are you real?	Obedience	Build Relationship Be a good listener Be authentic
Teens: *Thirteen to nineteen* Who am I? Can I be in charge?	Self-Respect	Give Responsibility Enable self-discovery Transfer accountability

While there are no guarantees with parenting—for children ultimately make their own choices—don't ever forget that your children will benefit from your example as much as from your training:

+ If you treat your spouse with respect, your children are more likely to respect both of you and follow that pattern in their relationships.

+ If you manage your money well, your children will learn the value of a dollar.

✦ If you appreciate people of all races, your children will be more likely to grow up without prejudice.

✦ If you handle losing well, your children will be equipped to lose well too.

✦ If you can laugh at your own mistakes, your children will better be able to laugh at their imperfections.

✦ If you accept tough jobs as challenges to be overcome, your children will be better equipped to fight their way through to complete their assignments.

✦ If you choose not to drink and drive, your children will most likely model your behavior.

Respect for parents, God, and others becomes respect for self and results in a respectful young adult. Are you doubtful you can instill this respect in your child? Don't be. Keep reading . . . you can raise children who graduate with honors from the School of Respect . . . you just need to be a willing coach!

Thirty-Six Ways to Cultivate a House of Respect

1. Pray together.
2. Say, "You're precious."
3. Tuck 'em in bed.
4. Hug, hug, and hug.
5. Say, "I love your eyes."
6. Sing, "Good morning."
7. Sing, "Good night."
8. Cut toast into heart shapes.
9. Say, "I love seeing your face every morning."
10. Tuck a love note in a lunchbox or a briefcase.
11. Have patience, patience, patience.
12. Look, learn, and love.
13. Put yourself in the other person's shoes.
14. Speak as respectfully to your spouse as you do to your boss.
15. Fly a kite together.
16. Love your kids enough to discipline.
17. Listen with your heart.
18. Show your kids how much you love your wife.
19. Show your kids how much you love your husband.
20. Draw a smiley face with syrup on your child's pancakes.
21. Give a backrub without being asked.
22. Polish your spouse's shoes.
23. Pray together.
24. Give something to every person who asks for help.
25. Preach less; love more.
26. Offer to read your child a book before you're asked.
27. Listen with your eyes.
28. Call just to say, "I love you."
29. Answer questions.
30. Say, "I'm sorry."
31. Clean your spouse's car.
32. Polish your child's bicycle.
33. Write a letter to your child, and send it through the mail.
34. Say, "Thank you."
35. Watch their favorite TV show.
36. Pray together.

4

Stress Purpose, Not Performance

ACROSS THE COUNTRY, hunting season follows on the heels of hurricane season, but a few brave men and women have earned the right to hunt whenever and wherever nature calls. This unique group of hunters chases down the most terrifying of beasts, known for the destruction their stampede leaves behind.

With the beast in sight, these expert marksmen take aim and fire up the engines of their WP-3Ds, GIV-SPs, and WC-130s. Into the "belly of the beast" they disappear, only to reappear hours later unscathed from the hunt.

The Hurricane Hunters, a rare breed of pilots, go above and beyond the call of duty with every flight. Manning one of only twelve specially equipped planes in the world, they fly directly into hurricanes, collecting valuable data that is helping hurricane forecasting become more of an exact science. In the past seven years, the hurricane landfall error forecast has dropped from 450 miles of coastline to approximately 150. At an estimated cost in excess of $1 million per mile to activate emergency services, the intangible savings to the American public have been substantial.[1]

Asking Hurricane Hunters, who are willing to die for what they do, why they do it brings a variety of answers, all with one central theme: purpose. Lieutenant Commander Cathy Martin says, "We do this for a reason . . . We're supporting our nation, and we're making sure that people get the information they need, so that if a storm's coming to the United States, they can get out of harm's way, by providing them with as much advance notice as possible."[2]

Keesler Air Force base in Biloxi, Missisipi, home to this elite unit, suffered severe damage in Katrina. Despite personal losses, the unit never missed a tasking from the National Hurricane Center. Its men and women carried out their duties without hesitation, putting service above self.

We want our children to become "expert marksmen" at what they do, so they can impact the world for good. We must be careful that our motives behind that desire are pure . . . to help our children become their best. God has a purpose for each of our children. You have been handed a mission. Are you willing to fly into the eye of the storm and help your children become all God created them to be?

Experience the Flight!

Just for fun, you and your children might enjoy climbing aboard a WC-130 with a Hurricane Hunter as he flies into the eye of a hurricane. Witness firsthand what these courageous pilots are willing to do for all of us. To experience the flight, type in this link: http://flightscience.noaa.gov/virtual_hunt.html.

In this chapter, we'll look at what happens when children are pushed to *perform* rather than encouraged to find God's *purpose* for their lives. This way, we will be able to avoid the same trap.

✳   ✳   ✳

AS HER THIRD CHILD ENTERED rehab, a mom well into her fifties commented, "I'm beginning to understand that my husband and I had something to do with this."

Let me give you a little history. Their daughter became pregnant at nineteen following a one-night stand with a guy who was present at the moment. Their son started his spiral in middle school with pot, then pills. By high school, his "I don't care" attitude turned from resentment to rebellion. If that wasn't enough, the angelic second daughter decided to ditch the halo and follow in her brother's footsteps. Three out of three troubled kids.

These parents are a well-educated, envied dream couple, committed Christians involved in their local church and missions and regular members of a Bible study group. But the warning signs were there: overindulgence coupled with pushing, not parenting. Their lives were all about performance. Growing up, the kids were often told, "I'm the best at what I do, and you should be the best at what you do." The dad was a charter member of AAOA (All-American Overachievers Association). He worked incessantly and expected his kids to do the same. It was all about numbers, ranking, position. In addition to her professional status as an attorney, the mom was an accomplished musician who settled for nothing less than perfection.

Before you peg them, there's a strange (but not uncommon) twist to this story. It wasn't just the expectations of these parents that hurt their children; it was the lack of expectations in the thing that mattered most . . . helping their children find their place in the family and their purpose in life. The parents pushed and coddled at the same time. They expected their kids to perform because of who they are, but did not help them find who they were meant to be. They expected their children to achieve greatness, but were not helping them become great. It was performance at all costs.

As long as they performed, the children could have whatever they wanted materially. They didn't have chores at home, so they didn't feel part of a family. The parents were so consumed with "doing the right things" that they devoted little time to getting to know their children's personalities and their hearts' desires. It is important to see the great irony in their parenting: pushing too hard while expecting too little.

The parents were lost in their mirrors. They could see who they had become and wanted clones of themselves. Until the second daughter fell by the wayside, they had not examined their role in the actions of their lost daughter and older son. They had blamed the school, their children's hanging out with the wrong friends, the lackluster youth program at church. The children themselves were blamed. You name the group, it had been given blame.

> It's not about **winning;** it's the joy of competition and being blessed with the opportunity to do what I love. I've never been one to project myself as Number One—I just go out and do the best that I can with what God has given me.
> —Coach Payton Jordan (1917–2009)

Maybe they will do a better job with their grandson, who is now living in the same house his mom grew up in.

Janine Bempechat, associate professor of human development at Wheelock College, has done extensive work in the area of adolescent development. She has concluded:

> The overriding concern parents have in setting expectations is their children's future success. But those expectations can have a negative effect if parents don't teach children the lessons they need to negotiate life. It's those life lessons—not academic knowledge or recreational skills, but qualities like diligence, perseverance, and responsibility—that will have the greatest effect on their lives. Parents need to remember that making sure their children acquire those skills is more

important in the long run than whether a child gets an A on a report card or wins a swimming meet.[3]

Parents who want to raise respectful children need to pay attention to these words. Before we attempt to help our kids in their endeavors, we need to step back and examine our motives. We've got a tough question to ask ourselves that will determine whether we are inspiring our kids out of a heart of love or pushing them out of a heart filled with selfish ambition.

Define Your Goal

ASK YOURSELF THESE DEFINING QUESTIONS: Do I want my child to be Number One? Or do I want my child to be the best he or she can be? In other words, don't ask what you want your child to do; instead, ask who you want your child to become. The answers to these questions will determine in which direction you'll lead and how you'll lead.

There's a stark contrast between the choices. One is about performance; the other, purpose. Take a look at the chart below as you ponder your answer:

NUMBER ONE	vs. THE BEST YOU CAN BE
Success	Significance
Short-term	Long-term
Room for compromise	No room for compromise
Covers mistakes	Rectifies mistakes
Gives up	Perseveres
Competes with others	Competes with self
Self-centered	Others-centered
Receives awards	Receives rewards

Parents who want their kids to be Number One focus on what their kids do, on their performance. The goal is short-term—win this match, win first place, be class valedictorian—with little thought for what kinds of adults the children will become. Parents who push their kids to be Number One often push so intensely that some kids are willing to cover up their mistakes and compromise to ensure they make it to the top. Others burn out or give up.

According to Dr. Michelle Kees of the University of Michigan:

> We see middle-school children who are already worrying if their grades are good enough for college, and teens entering high school whose primary focus is their college application. It's no longer about volunteering in order to make a difference; it's volunteering so their college application looks different. It's no longer about taking achievement tests to show what you know; it's to show where you are in the class. And this emphasis certainly has to have an impact on children.
>
> The drive to succeed should be in balance with a child's capabilities. We see some adolescents who are burning out. In the middle of their sophomore, junior, or senior year, their interest in school dissipates, their focus and concentration and drive start to fade. We see average students who are pressured to achieve above and beyond what they're capable of, or where their best interest lies.[4]

Those kids who don't drop out often grow up looking at life as a competition that they *have* to win. Worst of all, kids who grow up being told that winning is the only thing are more likely to grow up to become driven, self-centered adults. Sure, they may win awards, but these are fleeting, as their hearts are not full of the qualities needed to negotiate life—diligence, perseverance, respect for self and others, and responsibility, to name a few.

But character-centered parents who want their children to be the best they can be are concerned about helping their children live up to God's purpose for their lives—living up to their God-given potential. As we've discussed earlier, who your children become should be more important than what they do.

Jesus is the greatest example of someone who lived with purpose, who reached His potential. In the Garden of Gethsemane, He reached His potential to become the Savior of the world when He confessed, "Not my will, but thine, be done."[5] He reached the pinnacle of His purpose for walking among us when He went to the cross to save us from eternal separation from God. Jesus lived with the end in mind.

Character-centered parents make decisions with the end in mind—raising their children to become respectful adults who reach their God-given potential—so they encourage their children to correct their mistakes and rectify their wrongs. They inspire their kids to keep striving to reach their full potential and to persevere in the face of setbacks.

Kids raised with this kind of parenting are more likely to grow up to become adults who reach out to the world and make a difference in the lives of others. Their hearts are full of the "right stuff"—a long-lasting reward.

Never forget that your children are a part of you. They know the real you. They know your motives. They know if you're proud that they tried their best, even though they weren't the best player on the team, or if you're disappointed because they're not like another child who's faster and more adept. They know if winning matters more to you than their best effort.

"Winning isn't everything; it's the only thing" may have worked on the football field for the Green Bay Packers and Vince Lombardi, but it's a poor philosophy of life—and it certainly doesn't belong in the home. If winning is the only thing that matters to you, you may produce winners on the field but lose them off the field.

An Important Life Lesson

SEVERAL YEARS AGO, I WATCHED with great interest a high school track coach at a state meet. The incident I witnessed serves as a reminder of the importance of keeping your focus on competing with yourself, not on your competition.

The state championship rested on the outcome of the final race. As the runners neared the finish line, the lead runner made the serious mistake of glancing over his left shoulder and then his right. As he turned his head back to look ahead, the runner in the left lane leaned into the rope to take the race. The second-place finisher was devastated. Afterward the coach took him aside to have a private chat, which is impossible in the middle of a track stadium. The conversation went something like this:

COACH: Son, how many times have I told you, never take your eye off the mark. It doesn't matter what the other runners are doing. You're out there to run your best, regardless of what anyone else is doing.

RUNNER: But, Coach, I needed to know where my competition was.

COACH: Why?

RUNNER: Why? 'Cause . . . um . . . um . . . I don't know why.

COACH: Exactly . . . that's because it doesn't matter. It only matters how well you're running. If you concentrate on beating yourself, you don't have to worry about the competition.

Everyone present that day learned a life lesson: it doesn't matter what anyone else is doing.

Twelve years later, this high school track coach earned the 2012

Gill Athletics National High School Coach of the Year Award for boys' track and field. The award is given by Gills Athletics and USA Track & Field. What did Coach Claney Duplechin have to say?

> I'm thrilled to be in the presence of past winners and the other coaches nominated for this award. It's a great honor for me, but this isn't about just me. I've had so many great athletes and assistant coaches who share part of this.[6]

Head of School Hugh McIntosh said of Duplechin in a school news release, "Early on, he developed high standards in an enviable competitive spirit. He is a great coach, but more than that, I don't know a better man."[7]

Coach Duplechin's athletes have made 334 appearances at state outdoor championships. He has coached sixty-three state champions, including eleven pole vaulters, nine 1,600-meter runners, and eight champions each in the 800-meter and 3,200-meter races. He lives and teaches that the only person you compete with is yourself.

You're not competing with your neighbors. Your children aren't competing with the other kids in their class. Motivational speaker Zig Ziglar urges, "What you get by achieving your goals is not as important as what you become by achieving your goals."[8]

If you've raised your kids to be the best they can be, they are on their way to fulfilling their purpose, which is the ultimate way to help them "feel good about themselves," as we so often hear today. Rather than stressing performance, stress purpose. Help your children discover the reason they're here so that they can live up to their God-given potential.

How to Stress Purpose, Not Performance

GOD CREATED EACH OF YOUR children with talents, abilities, and a unique personality to form a one-of-a-kind human being who can make a difference in this world. Your job as parent is to help your kids become their best selves, so they can fulfill their God-given purpose. Here are some suggestions to get you started.

Help Kids Uncover Their Strengths and Weaknesses

IT'S NOT ALWAYS EASY TO uncover the strengths and weaknesses of your children. Make an effort in the early years to offer opportunities for exploration of the gifts that God has given your children. They can't always identify their strengths—that's why you must be intentional in looking for opportunities that enable them to find their interests:

+ *Expand your children's world as much as possible.* The more your children visit museums, the better. We lived in New York City when the boys were four years old. There were days when we stayed in the Metropolitan Museum from opening to closing. My sons have an appreciation of art that far exceeds most of my friends' interest or knowledge.

+ *Expose them to good books.* Read a long classic, little by little to your children when they are young. You'll fill their minds with possibilities and dreams of other places.

+ *Read them biographies* of people from many walks of life, from great artists to statesmen to missionaries to military generals, folks that made a difference in their fields and in the world.

✦ *Spend time in the great outdoors.* Watch how your children react. Are they comfortable sleeping under the stars or fearful? Are they at home with the sounds of the woods or ready to go home as soon as you get there?

✦ *Encourage your kids to get a taste of many different activities before they settle into one or two.* It's okay for elementary school children to try all the sports their school offers or to try playing a variety of musical instruments. Once they reach fourth or fifth grade, they begin to zero in on their areas of greatest interest. It's now time to settle on one or two activities per school year.

✦ *Involve them in craft activities and art projects.* Such activities will reveal any hidden artistic talent. Does your child enjoy the easy projects, or does she prefer a challenge? Does she become easily frustrated, or does she have an abundance of patience to complete a project?

✦ *Support their interests.* If your child enjoys art, set up an art corner in your home to encourage the budding artist. If your child enjoys nature, enroll him in programs that offer outdoor activities.

As you provide your kids with opportunities like the ones above, look for a pattern to emerge. What kinds of things is each child interested in? In what areas does each excel? What things give each child joy?

> Don't bother to be **better** than your contemporaries or predecessors. Try to be better than yourself.
> —William Faulkner

Although it is never a good idea to compare your children, looking at their differences can reveal their individual strengths. I was blessed with an ongoing study in my home through my identical twin sons. It was fascinating to watch Chad's leadership skills, as he tended to overpower Boyce much of the time. Boyce, on the other hand, displayed the qualities of a good negotiator, as he was willing to compromise for the sake of peace. Chad had a strong eye for color and proportion along with a keen mathematical sense. Boyce was a highly creative thinker and problem solver.

Because I had observed these qualities in my sons, I steered Chad toward architecture, which would allow him to use his sense of design and analysis. I encouraged Boyce to pursue entrepreneurship, so he could enjoy his gift of creative thinking.

So what fields did they choose in college? Chad earned a degree in economics and obtained a commercial real-estate license. Boyce earned a business degree in entrepreneurship. Good matches for both.

God has blessed your kids with specific talents and gifts to fulfill a specific purpose. When you help them identify those talents, you help them find their purpose.

Encourage Stickability by Helping Your Kids Keep the Big Picture in Mind

THE *AMERICAN HERITAGE DICTIONARY* DEFINES *persevere* as to "persist in or remain constant to a purpose, idea, or task in the face of obstacles or discouragement; and *perseverance* as steadfastness."[9] Using this definition as a basis, would you agree that perseverance can be defined as stubbornness with a purpose? It's not just refusing to give up; rather, it's refusing to give up *for a reason*. People who persevere have a passion behind their persistence. They have a dream, and when they bolster that dream through discipline, they persevere. Perseverance happens when dreams meet discipline. It's working not for gain, but for reward. Perseverance enables your child to succeed for the right reasons.

My mother believed you could reach your goals if you "use your abilities and stick to the task at hand." She taught us to set a goal and let nothing deter us from reaching it. We called her brand of perseverance "stickability."

"Don't quit," she would say. "Victory is within reach. Just keep reaching." Her words were powerful because she lived what she preached.

> Let us not grow weary while doing **good**, for in due season we shall reap if we do not lose heart.
>
> —Galatians 6:9 NKJV

My mother began working as a sales clerk in a downtown store to supplement her family's income when she was eleven years old. (I know, I know . . . but this was long before child-labor laws, and I'm not so certain Mother was truthful about her age.) Even though she was poor, she made a wise decision with her first wage of fifty cents that became a lifelong habit. She gave a nickel to the church, saved ten cents, and used the rest for necessities.

She encouraged my brother, sisters, and me to do the same. When we received our first allowance of twenty-five cents a week, each of us saved a nickel, gave a nickel to the church, spent ten cents on necessities, and spent the last nickel on something fun. (Mother *was* reasonable.) Every time we saved a dollar in coins, we could cash them in for a crisp, green dollar bill. When we approached Mother with a handful of coins, she would say, "See . . . money *does* grow on trees, if you plant the right seeds."

My mother had a purpose in mind for the money she earned— to give it away. She didn't earn money in order to buy for herself, but in order to buy for others. She didn't have "wants" like the rest of us. She met her needs and then looked for ways to help meet the needs of others. (At the tender age of eighty-four, my mother now gives away more money than she keeps.)

You can teach your kids a similar lesson by having them make a money tree. Not only is this a great way to teach stickability, it can also be a lesson in priorities and money management. As your children collect their coins, remind them they're planting valuable seeds. Discuss the importance of keeping their priorities straight. Help them establish a budget for the money they save. If they spend their change on trivial things, children learn quickly that they won't be able to "grow" the big dollars. When they come to you with a dollar in coins, use my mother's phrase, "Money does grow on trees when you plant the right seeds." It's all about setting your priorities with a bigger purpose in mind.

It will take all the perseverance you can muster to teach your children stickability. But if they are going to grow up to fulfill their potential, they'll need stickability and perseverance. So encourage and per-

---

Money Tree

You'll need Mod-Podge®, Plaster of Paris®, a bundle of paper money, medium-size sponge brushes, four-inch pots and six-inch saucers.

Pour Mod-Podge in a small plastic bowl. Help your children glue pieces of paper money to the pots using the sponge brushes and glue until covered. Let dry. Paint the entire pots with a thin layer of Mod-Podge and let dry again. Mix Plaster of Paris according to directions. Fill each pot to the bottom of the rim. Allow to stand for twenty to thirty minutes. Push a small branch into each pot and allow to harden overnight. Cover top of plaster with a little sheet moss or Easter grass.

Tell the children my mother's story of saving money. Encourage them to put one of the trees in their room and place their coins in the saucer until they save a dollar. When they cash in their coins for a crisp bill, hang the money on the tree.

Money really does grow on trees when you plant the right seeds!

suade, all the while being careful that in encouraging perseverance, you don't cross the line by expecting perfection.

Guard Against Perfectionism

SEEKING PERFECTION IS NOT THE same as seeking perseverance. Perseverance is striving to do the best you can do, even while knowing you can never be perfect. Why do we insist on perfection in our children when we ourselves will never be perfect?

You've witnessed the mom who says to her ten-year-old, average-size daughter, "No snacks for you. You're getting a little plump around the edges." Or the father who says to his son, "You'll get it right next time," after his son placed second in a race. Often parents who aggressively push their children propel them right into perfectionism. Perfectionism can actually keep children from achieving their potential. The message that comes through loud and clear to kids is that nothing less than perfect is of any value.

Have you caught yourself "helping" your son do an art project? Do you remake your daughter's bed after she has made it up? Do you wipe the counter again after the kids cleaned the kitchen? I can ask you these things because I committed these wrongs against my sons. I'm a classic perfectionist who has to work daily to overcome the irrational expectations I have of myself and others.

Your child could be headed down the destructive path of perfectionism if he or she:

+ Has unreasonable personal expectations

+ Is never satisfied with projects

+ Is critical of others

+ Has trouble making decisions

+ Falls apart when criticized

+ Procrastinates out of fear of failure

+ Is self-critical

If you recognize your child in this list, you can prevent perfectionism from becoming a lifelong malady by offering your child unconditional, accepting love.

In addition:

+ Stop the "nothing is ever quite good enough" attitude.

+ Accept your child for who he is, and help him grow into his potential.

+ Remember what it was like to be your child's age. So what if the juice is spilled or there are misspelled words in your first-grader's paper? Mishaps and mistakes are part of growing up.

+ When your child is disappointed by her shortcomings, share stories of times when you "messed up."

+ Don't compare your child with siblings or classmates.

+ Encourage your child to be his best, and let him know that's good enough for you.

One of the most obvious characteristics of perfectionists is the lack of downtime in their lives. Most perfectionists are serious-minded, driven folks who've forgotten the value of just playing around. Kids can get caught in this self-defeating trap. It's your job to make sure that doesn't happen.

Allow for Play

TWELVE-YEAR-OLD STEPHANIE COLLAPSED WHEN SHE walked through the back door of her home one afternoon. She couldn't take it anymore. Tears filled her eyes. Her mom's attempts at consoling her were in vain. Stephanie finally picked herself up and headed for her bedroom. A half-hour later her mom found her fast asleep, cradling a stuffed bunny from her toddler days.

Between dance, volleyball, study group, and school, Stephanie was exhausted. How did her schedule get so out of control? Because her mom forgot the importance of unstructured playtime, even for older children.

For young children, play is their work. Attributes that lead to success, such as patience, getting along with others, and problem-solving are best learned while kids are just being kids. Have you ever watched how a group of kids on the playground interact? Stock traders could learn a lot about the art of negotiation by watching the give-and-take of eight-year-olds as they play a game of kickball.

Children at play feel safer trying new things around peers rather than around parents because the level of expectation is lower, and as a result, it heightens their curiosity and creativity. Children who can't seem to focus in structured settings are able to concentrate when it comes to play. Kids who play hard on the playground may transfer that energy into seeking their potential later in life.

Some additional life skills gained during playtime include:

> The job of a football **coach** is to make men do what they don't want to do, in order to achieve what they've always wanted to be.
>
> —Tom Landry

+ Ability to make choices and decisions based on what's best for all

✦ Perseverance

✦ Ability to encourage others

✦ Ability to find joy in others' accomplishments (which is too often lost in the classroom or on the sports field)

✦ Strategic planning

✦ Ability to express ideas

Parents who allow their kids lots of time for free play are equipping them with the important skill sets they need to succeed and fulfill their potential. When children play name games, sing songs, and recite jump-rope rhymes, they're developing language skills. When they construct a block tower, follow directions to a game, and figure out pieces to a puzzle, they're developing thinking skills. When they string beads, make clay figures, and cut with scissors, they're developing small-muscle skills; and they develop large-muscle skills when they play ball, roller-skate, and run relay races. When they make up stories, put on a puppet show, and play dress-up, they are nurturing skills in creativity. When they team up to play ball games, discuss rules for a card game, and decide who will play what part in a dramatic play, they are developing their social skills.

The value of play is priceless. When they are being silly and laughing, children receive the refueling they need to meet the challenges of growing up.

Encourage a Close Relationship with God

WHEN OUR CHILDREN DEVELOP A close relationship with God, they begin on their own to want to please Him. In so doing, they'll naturally desire and work toward fulfilling God's call on their lives and reaching their full potential. How can you help your children cultivate a relationship with God? In large part by showing the power of prayer.

Teaching children to pray is easy if you are a praying parent. Your children will discover the joy of prayer through your prayers, so:

+ *Pray before every meal.* If you do, by the time they're age three, your kids will be asking you if they can pray before you have a chance to ask them—and they will embrace this habit for themselves. It doesn't matter where we are or who is with us; before we begin a meal, one of my grown sons reaches across the table to take the hand of whoever he's with to offer grace. And it's not a rote prayer, but words from the heart. "Saying grace" is the most basic of all prayers.

+ *Allow your kids to "catch" you talking to God during the day.* If they do, they will learn to rely on prayer not just for the big things, but the little things too.

+ *Let them see you on your knees in prayer.* This will help them understand God's majesty and holiness.

+ *Let them hear you tell others that you'll pray for them.* Your kids will be more likely to develop a desire to pray for others too.

+ *Talk with them about answers to prayer for your family.* This teaches your children that God does answer prayer.

You're probably familiar with the classic book *Goodnight Moon* by Margaret Wise Brown. For more than fifty years, this book has encouraged children to find comfort in telling the moon good night. I'd like to encourage you to instill another "good night" habit in your children. When your kids are young, encourage them to say, "Good night, Lord" as you tuck them in bed after night-night prayers.

When they awaken, kiss them, and remind them to say, "Good morning, Lord." This is a beautiful, holy habit that teaches children to talk to God before the day begins and as it comes to a close.

If you fail at all other points but accomplish the task of instilling a desire to talk to God in your children, you will have still equipped them with the best tool to discover their purpose.

(The search for purpose in your child's life starts with you and ends with God.)

5

Coach; Don't Cheerlead

O FTEN LAUDED FOR its quick responsiveness and flexibility in a broad range of emergencies, the Coast Guard was the shining star in the search and rescue efforts following Katrina. Within hours of Katrina's landfall, Coast Guard crews moved in. The work was dangerous and demanding. Pilots hovered between electrical wires and dropped cables 180 feet. Rescue swimmers dove into muddy contaminated water with no foreknowledge of what they would encounter. Technicians became boat pilots. Small boat operators became urban police officers.

David Young, one of the Coast Guard technicians turned rescuers, said, "Myself and nine other junior service members jumped into the fire not knowing what to expect. But like the Coast Guard has done for hundreds of years, we adapted and overcame."[1] Machinery Technician Young and his team members did what they were trained to do: adapt and overcome.

The smallest of the military branches, the Coast Guard has

been involved in every war since the Civil War, but combat is not its primary mission. The Coast Guard's main mission is to keep us safe from harm and secure within our borders. Personnel are trained to be team members who aspire to go above and beyond their call of duty. They are put through rigorous exercises that teach them how to think on their feet and problem-solve. They are deployed every day, not just in times of emergency. When disasters do occur, they can handle the pressure. They live up to their motto: *Semper Paratus*—"Always Ready."

The Coast Guard training reminds me of the training a parent should do with the home team. Inspiring each member to be his or her best for the good of the team. Giving team members the confidence and courage to do the seemingly impossible. Teaching members how to be adaptable to change when tough problems come along. Standing with family members when obstacles threaten to stop progress.

In this chapter, you'll be equipped to train your children with the precision of a Coast Guard coach. You can choose to be the one to inspire and encourage your children to be their best. You can help your children be "always ready" for whatever this disrespectful world chooses to blow their way. It's not that hard, really. It's just a matter of training with the right goal in mind . . . children who can adapt and overcome.

✳　✳　✳

CONSIDER THESE TWO SCENARIOS:

Scenario 1: The game's over. Johnny leaves his outfield position with his head so low you can see the button on the crown of his baseball cap. He'd struck out twice and missed a fly ball. He isn't sure which hurts more, his pride or his backside, from tripping over his own two feet when he went for the fly ball.

His mother is waiting for him as he mopes off the field. "Oh, Johnny, I'm so proud of you. You're the best player on the team. If all the guys could play like you, well . . . we'd be the state champions!"

"Mom, don't . . . don't say that."

But Mom continues, "Oh, Johnny, don't ever forget . . . you're the best!"

Scenario 2: The game's over. Johnny struck out twice and missed a fly ball because he tripped over his own two feet . . . in front of the coaches, parents, spectators, and his teammates. It was a crucial play—the win-or-lose moment—and he had blown it.

He can barely walk, much less hold his head up. His brain is telling his little bird legs to run—get out of there—but they don't want to move. His heart is aching, and his ego is wounded.

His mother greets Johnny as he finally makes it to the sidelines, the last player off the field. Squatting down to get eye-to-eye with her son, she says, "Oh, Johnny, tough game today. My heart hurt with yours when you struck out. And that fly ball, ugh . . . your feet just didn't cooperate, did they?"

Johnny looks into his mother's eyes and reaches for the warmth of her embrace as she continues. "I tell you what, Johnny. How about if this weekend I make some lemonade and those cookies everybody likes. We'll invite some of the older guys over and between Dad and the guys, you can work on your hitting and fly balls," she says with great empathy.

Johnny nods his head in agreement.

Then his mother adds, "If you keep working at it . . . you'll get it. It just takes practice. I know you can get it. Dad and I will help you."

* * *

IN THE FIRST SCENARIO, THE mother functions as a cheerleader. How do you think her words affected her son? At ten years old, Johnny knew he wasn't the best player on his team, and he knew he hadn't played well during the game. And unless his mother had left the game or somehow missed most of it, she had to know it too.

Here are a few possible responses that her words of false praise might have elicited in her son:

+ *Mom lied to me. How could she do that?* (His mother's words of false praise damaged his trust in her.)

+ *I messed up. Why didn't she care that I had a bad game?* (His mom's refusal to acknowledge what had really happened makes Johnny feel worse than he feels about how he played the game. Doesn't she care about him or even see him?)

+ *I know I'm not the best player on the team, but I love baseball. Why isn't it okay to just be part of the team?* (His mom's false praise gives Johnny the impression that he has to be the best. Anything less is not good enough.)

+ *I'll never be the best player on the team, so what's the use in trying?* (Since Johnny knows he'll never be the best, he gives up trying to improve.)

In the second scenario, Johnny's mom serves as his coach. She doesn't use false praise to try to make him feel better. Instead, she lets him know she understands how bad he feels and encourages him by telling him she's going to see that he gets help to improve his game. She doesn't deny reality but offers Johnny hope that he will perform better in the future.

As a result, her son likely had one or more of the following responses:

+ *Mom's the best. She really loves me.* (His mother sealed the bond with her son by joining in his disappointment. Her words told him his number-one fan felt his pain.)

✦ *I messed up, but Mom still loves me.* (Because she didn't sugarcoat his mistakes, Johnny knows his mom's love for him is not based on his performance.)

✦ *I'm glad Mom and Dad will help me. Maybe I can become a good player.* (His mom's offer to provide help gave Johnny hope that he can improve.)

✦ *I won't give up. I'll play better next week.* (His mom's encouragement gave Johnny the motivation to persevere, even in the face of disappointment.)

CHEERLEAD	vs.	COACH
Offers false praise		Offers genuine praise
Doesn't / can't offer instruction		Provides expertise
Uses external motivation		Uses internal motivation
Applauds mediocrity		Expects excellence

In the rest of this chapter we are going to take a closer look at why it's so important that parents not take on the role of cheerleader, and then we'll discuss how you can be the coach your kids need in order to grow up to become respectful adults.

Don't Cheerlead

PERHAPS YOU'RE STILL WONDERING WHAT'S so bad about being a cheerleader parent. After all, what's so bad about telling kids they're great?

If you think about it, the reason will quickly become evident. Cheerleaders can't help their team win. All cheerleaders do is keep yelling about how great their team is—even when the scoreboard and stat sheet paint a very different picture. Cheerleader moms try to boost their children's flagging spirits in the face of an athletic defeat, a low test score, or a disappointing placement in a contest, but they don't do anything to equip their children to do better next time.

When a parent praises a child who has done nothing to earn that praise, the praise is false because it's not based upon fact. Consider these examples:

- A ten-year-old wants to take drum lessons. His mom says: "Oh, sweetheart, you're so talented, you don't need lessons."

- A sixteen-year-old is in tears because of her acne. Her mom tells her, "Your face is beautiful."

- A high school freshman hands her mom her report card, which is filled with C's. Her mom smiles and says, "Honey, it's okay. We know you're the smartest kid in your class."

- After hearing his seven-year-old play the piano after just one lesson, his dad says, "I can't imagine you could play any better."

- After attending a speech contest in which his daughter stumbled over words and forgot her closing, the dad tells his daughter, "You're the very best I've ever heard."

Parents who say things like these to their kids may be well intentioned, but their words hurt rather than help. Let me show you why.

False Praise Diminishes Trust

KIDS KNOW WHEN THEY HAVE done well and when they haven't. We cannot erase the pain of defeat by telling them they did well. We also lose an opportunity to strengthen our relationship with them, because our disingenuousness shakes their trust in us. When we acknowledge they didn't do well, we are telling our children we feel their pain, and we gain a deeper level of trust because they know they can count on us to tell them the truth about themselves with love.

We all have friends who flatter us. You know the kind I'm talking about—female friends who tell you your new hairstyle is the best one you've ever had, your new hair color takes ten years off your face, or you look slimmer in the dress that's a size too small. Men do it too—Tom might tell Jim his tie is "right in style" even though the tie doesn't match his shirt. While these friends may mean well, you likely don't go to them when you want an honest answer.

When I really want to know the truth, good or bad, I turn to my friend Jean. Why? Because experience has taught me that she'll tell me the truth, the whole truth, and nothing but the truth . . . even when it's hard to take. So Jean is the one I turn to when I need an honest opinion about matters more important than my hairstyle. I trust her and her judgment of me. She has never offered false praise; she always offers help.

Here's the tough truth: false praise (I like to call it junk praise) is a lie. Telling your children they're the best when they're not is a lie, plain and simple. Remember, a child's world is black and white; there's no gray. Your words are either true or they are false—there are no half-truths. So when cheerleader parents offer unwarranted praise to their children, the kids will hear it as a lie. Instead of helping the child feel better, false praise causes kids to lose their trust in their parents because they wonder, *what else are my parents lying to me about?*

You were meant to be the one your child turns to when she

needs someone she can really trust. Whether she's five years old and just lost her best friend on the playground or fifteen and feeling like a failure because she wasn't chosen for the homecoming court, she needs to know she can trust you to tell her the truth about herself. She needs you to acknowledge something painful has happened and that you understand how she feels.

For example:

✦ With your five-year-old, you might say, "I know how much it hurts when you lose a friend. Let's talk about what happened and see if both of you might need to say, 'I'm sorry.' Come on, I'll push you on the swing while we talk."

✦ When your fifteen-year-old's ego is bruised, you might say, "Not every girl in your class can be on the home-coming court. Maybe Cindy just knows more of the kids than you do—she is dating a football player. And you're trying out for the play in the spring, aren't you?"

But loss of trust isn't the only consequence when parents give kids false praise.

False Praise Undermines Ambition

DR. JEAN TWENGE, AN ASSISTANT professor of psychology at San Diego State University, reports, "This generation has given up. We're looking at 'Generation Whatever,' with many kids feeling like they can't make a difference."[2] In our quest to help our children feel good about themselves (gain self-esteem), we shower them with false praise because we don't want them to feel bad. But for words of praise to inspire and motivate, they must be warranted.

False praise stifles motivation to improve. If we tell our children,

"You're the best," what's to improve? False praise can lead to a false assumption about their ability, causing a child not to get the help or instruction needed to reach his or her potential. Somewhere along the line, these kids will find out the truth about themselves.

Parents destroy their children's ambition when they shower them with false praise and then make excuses for their lack of achievement. That's what Billy's mom did. She told him his singing was fabulous and that he was going to be a star. He quit his voice lessons because he was tired of the vocal exercises and felt his instructor was too rigid. A few months later when Billy tried out for the spring musical and didn't receive a part, his mom played the blame game, telling people:

"Joey beat Billy for the lead because his dad works with the director . . . that has to be the reason."

"Billy's voice was scratchy from all the singing he's been doing at church."

"This play is small potatoes for Billy. He's trying out for a part in the community theater next month anyway."

If children lack ambition, they won't keep striving to become more than they are today. As a result they won't develop self-respect, because they haven't experienced the confidence that comes from setting a goal and achieving it through hard work and perseverance.

If parents only tell their kids how wonderful and beautiful and smart they are, their children will grow up believing it and also expecting the world to tell them the same thing. Rather than doing things out of a healthy, internal motivation of self-respect or concern for others, these kids are motivated by what others think of them. They want to be in the limelight, and when they aren't, they get confused and don't know what to do.

I saw this when my sons graduated from high school. Several of their peers, who had excelled in high school, suddenly seemed to fall by the wayside. When they no longer received weekly accolades telling them how great they were, they didn't know what to do. They didn't go to college or pursue careers. They were left without support or direction, because the false motivating praise that got them through high school had never been internalized and transformed into self-respect.

False Praise Fails to Offer Guidance

CHEERLEADER PARENTS TEND TO FEEL good about themselves as parents because they are saying nice things to their kids, trying to make them feel good about themselves; but they stop short of offering what their children really need: guidance. For example, they say things like:

+ It's not your fault you failed."

+ "I don't know why your coach won't let you start. You're his best player."

+ "Oh, darling, you're so beautiful. You can't win them all."

+ "Forget about it; you'll make the goal next week."

While encouraging words like these may affirm kids when they are disappointed in themselves, they miss the mark because they fail to offer guidance, which is what the kids really need. Cheering won't ensure our children's victories—only hard work does that. Victory in sports, and in life, grows out of how prepared we are. Victory grows out of training.

It's not enough to tell our kids we believe in them and that they can do anything they want. They need us to guide them, to show them how to do what they want or need to do. This was brought home to me when my sons turned twelve and were old enough to mow our lawn. One day I announced that I believed they were now mature enough, smart enough, strong enough, and tough enough to handle the job. After this ego-building speech, we headed for Sears to purchase a power mower. When we got back home, I helped them fill the tank, started it up, and told them to start mowing. I went back in the house and left them in the backyard. Thirty minutes later Chad came bounding into the house, saying, "Mom, aren't you going to show us how to do it?"

"Darling, I gave you instructions. I know you can do it; you're smart enough," I replied.

Chad came right back at me, "But, Mom, you can't just tell us; you have to show us."

Once again, my son stopped me dead in my tracks with truth. Telling our children isn't enough; we have to show them, which is why kids need parents who are coaches rather than cheerleaders.

Good coaches do two things: they offer encouragement, and they coach by example.

Offer Encouragement

PAYTON JORDAN, THE FORMER OLYMPIC track coach who led the 1968 United States team to the gold in the Mexico City Olympics and coached Stanford's national championship teams for thirty years, was a great role model for parents who wanted to effectively coach their kids. Jordan's peers and team members referred to him as a "teacher, mentor, friend, hero, role model, leader, motivator, a master at creating self-respect, a man of rectitude, discipline, and integrity, and a national treasure."[3]

As I was researching this book, I contacted Coach Jordan, and we became good friends. As we talked about his training philosophy, he told me that encouragement lay at the heart of his coaching. Bob Moore, a former team member, agreed. "Coach Jordan had a talent for making you feel better about yourself and more confident in your ability to take on any challenge. He could look you straight in the eye and make you feel like you would climb mountains and swim through shark infested waters to meet his expectations of you . . . and then, the miracle of it all, was that those expectations became your expectations!"[4]

Words of Encouragement

Admonish, exhort, move, prompt, urge, incite, induce, persuade, gladden, brighten, hearten, pick up, inspire, elevate one's mood, give a lift, put one on top of the world, exhilarate, rejoice, do the heart good, enliven, console, give comfort, reassure, pat on the back, embolden, bolster, support, foster, nurture, and we could keep going . . .

I urge you to read through these words and phrases several times before you move on. Let each one sink into your heart.

Your encouragement or lack of encouragement can make or break your child's self-respect. What follows are concepts I've adapted from Payton Jordan's coaching philosophy. These concepts can aid parents in their efforts to raise respectful children.

Speak Words of Genuine Praise

WE ALL NEED A LITTLE praise, a pat on the back, for a job well done. When you acknowledge your children's accomplishments, you help build their self-image. Nothing feels better than knowing you did something well that was noticed, especially by someone you love and trust.

False praise can destroy motivation, but genuine praise can bolster it. When children receive genuine praise from their parents, they'll want to try harder; they'll long to live up to the expectations laid before them. So praise your kids when they accomplish a task. Encourage them to keep going with comments such as, "Boy, you're going to feel good when your teacher sees how hard you've worked on this science project," rather than saying, "I'm going to be so proud of you when you turn in this science project." Phrase your comments to focus on how the child will feel. This lets your child know your encouragement is for his or her good, not for your ego.

When your children do extra chores to earn money to buy a present for a grandparent, give away their favorite toy to a child who doesn't have a toy, or help a friend who's upset rather than going to the "party of the decade," remind them God is watching what they do—not to catch them doing something wrong, but to smile at them when they do something right. I call such moments "God winks." By the time they're teenagers, kids won't be doing a good job just for you; they'll be motivated by their desire to honor God.

Your goal is to move your child from depending on your encouragement for motivation to being self-motivated, and when parents provide genuine praise, they help their children make this move.

Build Their Character

"I DON'T WANT IT," EIGHT-YEAR-OLD Boyce complained, as he threw his baseball trophy on the floorboard of the car. "I hate baseball. I hate my coach. I hate this trophy."

When I got over the shock, I scolded Boyce with not-so-wise words: "Boyce, that's no way to talk about your coach and no way to treat your trophy. You should be grateful to your coach and proud of your trophy."

"Mom, you don't get it, do you?" he came back with a disrespect-ful pitch.

Obviously I was missing something. "Boyce, you'd better explain in a hurry, or we're going to have to do something about that rotten attitude," I answered in my most motherly tone.

"Mom, everybody gets one. It's no big deal," Boyce said as he slumped down on the seat with that pitiful little-boy look of disap-pointment.

He was right. It *was* no big deal. It didn't matter if he tried or not, if he ever hit the ball or not, because everybody on the team got a tro-phy for participation. No one was singled out for excellence. Don't misunderstand: Boyce wasn't upset because he thought he was the best player and deserved special recognition. Quite the contrary. He didn't feel he had earned the trophy, so he couldn't be thankful for it.

Participation in Little League sports used to be a character-building experience. Too often in today's sports programs we're more focused on coddling children than coaching them to excel-lence. We try to make all things equal by stroking our kids, but this ruins their ability to be grateful for their achievements. Here are some ways to help your kids develop character, which is what they really need:

+ *Don't make excuses for your child.* Rather than making excuses for your child's less-than-stellar performance, let him know you believe he can do better.

+ *Raise your expectations.* Don't lower them to accommo-date your child. Our kids will live up to our expectations when they're challenging but reasonable. Don't set your expectation on last-chair trumpet in the high school band when you know your child is capable of moving up. Encourage your child with extra lessons and your willingness to sit and listen to him practice.

✦ *Dream big with your child.* Help your child understand
that it doesn't matter where she is today; what matters is
where she's going to be tomorrow. A great conversation
starter with your child is to ask, "Who do you want to
become one day?" If the response is "the most famous
inventor in the world," tell your child stories of famous
inventors, such as Thomas Edison, who once said, "If I
find 10,000 ways something won't work, I haven't failed.
I am not discouraged, because every wrong attempt dis-
carded is often a step forward."[5]

Let your children know nothing worth achieving ever comes
easily.

Another coach whose philosophies can offer us helpful insights
into training our children fascinated me and most of America during a career that spanned almost thirty years. He showed us all how
to lead by example with integrity and consistency.

Coach by Example

WHEN I WAS IN HIGH school, the Dallas Cowboys dominated the
NFL, as did their coach, Tom Landry. Wearing his signature felt fe-
dora, he commanded his team from the sidelines with confidence
and cool that set the mark for other coaches in the league. Landry
was known as a man of few words, but the words he spoke were
important.

Known as "America's coach," Landry built the Dallas franchise
from the ground up, never deviating from his own priority list:
God, family, and football. (Sound familiar?) He wrote it on every
training-camp blackboard for twenty-nine years. I believe part of his

long-term success came from keeping his priority list in order.

Coach Landry's demeanor exuded confidence under pressure. He commanded control of his team because he had earned their respect. At Landry's memorial service in February 2000, one of his most successful players, Roger Staubach, with tear-filled eyes said, "He was our rock, our hope, our inspiration. He was our coach."[6]

What a great description of what it means to be your kids' coach! Be their rock, hope, and inspiration.

Be Their Rock

ROGER STAUBACH WASN'T THE FIRST to refer to Coach Landry as a rock. The media frequently called him the "Rock of Gibraltar." Why? Because Tom Landry was a man of character who never compromised his integrity. What a lesson for us as we seek to instill respect in our children: we must be the rock upon which their character is built.

I've said it before, and I'll say it throughout this book because it is so important: *kids follow their parents' example.* If you want to raise respectful kids, you need to be their rock. They need you to live a life of integrity born out of character that has been shaped by the principles found in God's Word.

Jesus said, "I will show you what he is like who comes to me and hears my words and puts them into practice. He is like a man building a house, who dug down deep and laid the foundation on rock. When a flood came, the torrent struck that house but could not shake it, because it was well-built."[7] Is your life a solid rock upon which your kids can build their belief system?

Someone once said, "A man who stands for nothing will fall for anything." Quite a contrast to Jesus's exhortation to build your life on the solid foundation of God's Word. What do you believe in? What do you stand behind? If you're not building your life on the solid foundation of God's Word, then you are standing on shifting sand, and so are your kids. Everyone is talking about spirituality today, of having faith in something. I tire of hearing "all that matters is that you believe in something." Not true. What matters is whether what we believe in is true.

A highly educated man once told me he had a recurring dream of being thrown into the ocean. The waves violently tossed him back and forth until he finally went under. Just when all hope was gone, he resurfaced for a saving breath of air, only to begin the torment again. I tried to help him see that this recurring dream represented the lack of a foundation of faith in his life. With all his education and worldly success, his soul was not anchored.

Scripture tells us that when we turn our hearts and minds to God, the sure foundation, "we will no longer be infants, *tossed back and forth* by the waves, and blown here and there by every wind of teaching and by the cunning and craftiness of men in their deceitful scheming."[8]

Your children need you to provide them with a solid foundation of trust in God and their parents. Your children need to know that your character and integrity are rock solid. They need to know that you:

+ Are not deceived by every new teaching that comes along

+ Are not persuaded to accept a contract from a company of questionable ethics, even though your partners don't have a problem with it

+ Are the one to dissent when your child's elementary

school wants to sell alcoholic beverages at the fall carnival to make more money, because it sends a mixed message to the children about alcohol consumption

✦ Run in the other direction when temptation comes in the form of another who is not your spouse, no matter the difficulties you're experiencing within your marriage

When parents don't compromise their integrity, they give their children the rock-solid foundation they need. Such parents provide a model for how their kids can develop a rock-solid foundation of their own.

A good coach also exemplifies hope.

Hang On to Hope

COACH LANDRY RACKED UP FOUR losing seasons in a row during his first years with the Cowboys. Even so, he was offered a ten-year contract to continue with the team because of his attitude and his determination to build a winning team. When asked about his unending optimism, he commented, "I've learned that something constructive comes from every defeat."[9] This perspective allowed him to offer hope to his team, and that hope enabled them to persevere. Hope provided the Cowboys with the motivation to keep on trying, and their efforts eventually took them to the top of the NFL, winning two Super Bowl championships, five NFC championships, and 270 victories.

Do your kids see hope in you when times get tough? Do you persevere, expecting a positive outcome? I'm not advocating naiveté; I'm talking about mature hope that stems from a rock-solid foundation of hope and trust in a sovereign God.

I learned a great lesson in hope when I decided to write *Man-*

ners of the Heart. After I'd sent off a proposal to numerous publishers, a writer friend told me, "It takes twenty-five rejections before you'll get an acceptance." I had a choice to make every time I found a rejection letter in the mailbox. I could see each letter as a crushing blow to my hope that one day I would be published, or I could see each rejection as bringing me one step closer to my goal. I chose the latter option. Together, the boys and I began celebrating each rejection letter as it arrived.

If you exemplify hope in the midst of difficulties and challenges, your daughter won't quit the first time she's humiliated on the soccer field or the fifth time she has to sit on the bench. Your son will keep trying for first chair in the school band and will spend more time practicing so he can one day achieve that goal. When our kids see us not giving up when we face defeat or rejection, we teach them to persist toward their own goals, to keep working toward mastery.

> *Love* . . . always protects, always trusts, always hopes, always perseveres.
>
> —1 Corinthians 13:6–7

Nothing is more gratifying to a parent than seeing evidence that our kids have "caught" what we have been trying to teach them. I worked hard to exemplify hope to my sons. That's why I was so excited the day Chad's own hope was rewarded.

Chad loved football and started playing in fourth grade, determined to one day become an outstanding player. But I knew he had little chance of this because his body simply refused to grow at the rate of his teammates. He was the kid who followed every play up and down the field, patting every player as he came back to the sidelines. He played with his heart, continuing to go out for the team in hopes that one day he would turn into the player of his dreams.

When summer football training started up each year, I'd tell Chad that maybe this year he was going to "pump up." I found "little" guys who had made it big in the NFL to use as examples of those who succeeded despite their size. I reminded Chad that his teammates appreciated his enthusiasm and needed his encouragement. I emphasized his contribution in each game, pointing out that even though his shining moment had not come yet, he was already an important member of the team because he gave so unselfishly while he continued to hope for the chance to prove himself.

In seventh grade, Chad's coach put him in the game. The opposing quarterback threw a long pass, and Chad caught the ball, right in front of the intended receiver. I was so proud of my son at that moment that I lost all dignity! But I wasn't the only one. The bench cleared. The whole team celebrated Chad's moment of glory. Why? Because they knew he had given his all to his team. Chad played with his heart, a heart filled with hope, and they wanted to rejoice with him when his hope did not return void.

Hope is the heartbeat of the family. Love your family enough to give them hope, no matter how difficult the circumstances.

And . . .

Be Their Inspiration

IN ONE OF OUR "BUSINESS of Manners"® training sessions, I ask the participants to record ten attributes they would like to see in an employee, and then we compile their answers into one list. Next, I ask if anyone in the room is the perfect employee in the company. When no one says yes, I challenge the attendees to make their lists a personal goal for themselves.

Let me challenge you to do something similar. What would the perfect parent coach look like to you? And more important, what qualities in you do you want your children to emulate? Answer that question, and then with God's help strive to live up to those qualities!

+ Do you want your children to be the best they can be? Then expect nothing less of yourself.

+ Do you want your kids to respect your word? Then keep your word.

+ Do you want them to tell the truth? Then always tell the truth. Don't sugarcoat it or tell half-truths.

+ Do you want your children to be unselfish? Then give generously to those in need.

+ Do you want them to persevere? Then don't give up when the going gets tough.

+ Do you want your kids to be faithful? Then keep your commitments.

+ Do you want them to have self-control? Then don't lose your control.

+ Do you want your children to be patient? Then endure irritations with grace.

+ Do you want them to respect others? Then show respect for others, beginning with your spouse. Fathers should teach their children to respect their mother. Mothers should teach their children to respect their father. Together you teach your children how to respect others.

If you live out the qualities on your list, you will inspire your kids to live that way as well. No one can be perfect, but we all can try to be a little better today than we were yesterday.

Do the Best You Can!

COACH JORDAN SAID IT BEST: "[Being a coach] means going out and doing the best you can with what God's given you."

If you take your coaching position with your children seriously, one day your children will say of you what one of Coach Jordan's former teammates said about him: "He was an outspoken proponent of old-fashioned values: a man of principle, of character, and of courage and determination."[10]

Coach Jordan passed away in 2009, leaving behind the memory of his "man-making ability."

6

Set Boundaries Without Building Walls

ARE YOU A cloud spotter? As a child, did you find Tyrannosaurus rex walking across the sky? Did you see a fish jumping out of water? Have you helped your children find the face of an angel peering through a cloud? Or maybe as an adult you've stared in wonder as storm clouds rolled in.

Conjure up the image of the low-hanging pouch-like clouds in the movies *Ghostbusters* or *Independence Day*. Interestingly enough, that type of cloud formation is called *mammatus*, derived from the Latin *mamma* (meaning "udder").[1] Because of "mamma's" menacing appearance, she is often seen as a harbinger of a coming storm or other extreme weather system. She can extend for hundreds of miles in each direction and remain visibly static for ten to fifteen minutes at a time. While she may appear foreboding, she is merely the messenger of the danger lurking—appearing around, before, or even after severe weather.[2]

While "mamma's" appearance signals impending severe weather, the deceptively beautiful "wall" cloud masks the formation of severe weather. Often within minutes of the appearance of a "wall" cloud, a twister will burst through and strike the closest target in sight. And what happens to "mamma"? She's there after the "wall" cloud dissipates to signal the storm has passed.

You know where I'm going with this one . . . It's Mamma's job, and Dad's job, to warn of impending danger by setting boundaries—the rules of the family that protect children from harm in all directions. Harm from the outside, "friends" who tempt toward wrongdoing. Harm from the inside, hearts that want what they want and want it now, at any cost. Harm from inexperience, immaturity that doesn't allow for wise decision-making yet.

Just as the "wall" cloud hides the horrific danger that lies behind it, when we put too many boundaries in place, we begin to lose opportunities to build a strong relationship with our children and instead begin building a wall between us. Our children can and will hide behind the wall. Deception sets in. Lies begin. Trust is lost.

In this chapter, you will learn how to set necessary boundaries for your children without allowing those boundaries of safety to become walls that separate you. Boundaries build trust. Walls create resentment and rebellion behind which an angry storm will brew.

> To find fascinating information and breathtaking photographs of cloud formations to share with your children, visit the Cloud Appreciation Society's website: www.cloudappreciationsociety.org.

* * *

SOME JUNIOR-HIGH STUDENTS HUDDLED AROUND the inside perimeter of a schoolyard fence. A passing psychologist from the local university noted this and subsequently suggested that the fences represented unwelcome limitations, and that children would do better with an unrestricted schoolyard. Thus the fences all came down. The result? The children began to huddle in the middle of the playground, because they did not know where the boundaries were.[3]

The boundaries we'll visit in this chapter are the rules for behavior that protect our children from disaster and communicate that someone in authority cares enough about them to provide direction and guidance. Kids need firm boundaries so they can get on with the task of growing up to be respectful and responsible.

When God created the Garden of Eden, He put boundaries in place for Adam and Eve's protection. God gave the Israelites the Ten Commandments so they would know what He expected in terms of their behavior—not for His good, but for the good of His children. As our heavenly Parent, He knows what's best for us—what will bring joy or sorrow, happiness or despair, blessing or burden. God wants us to provide the same guidance and protection for our children by setting boundaries, not for our comfort, but for our children's security.

Boundaries can help children:

+ Develop self-control and a sense of responsibility for their own behavior

+ Resist peer pressure and every new fad that comes along, dangerous or not

+ Understand that wrong behavior has negative consequences

+ Feel secure under the protection of parental authority

+ Know what's expected of them

+ Gain wisdom, knowledge, and guidance in a complicated world

Without a doubt, boundaries go a long way toward helping children develop the qualities they need to become respectful adults. So in this chapter we'll explore how you can set boundaries that help rather than hinder your children and that do not create walls between you and them, beginning with the importance of a unified front.

Present a Unified Front

AFTER TWENTY-EIGHT YEARS OF PARENTING, Mike and Lisa Conn, the character-centered parents you met in Chapter 2, have learned the importance of presenting a unified front to their girls, particularly when it comes to establishing and enforcing boundaries. This hasn't always been easy, though, because Mike and Lisa are opposite in almost every aspect of temperament and personality. They see life from different perspectives and have not always agreed on what's best for their daughters, Ali, Ashley, and Aimee. Through the years they've argued about whether or not the baby should wear a cap, how short their daughters' skirts should be, when to set curfews, and issues ranging from baby formulas to restaurant choices.

But in spite of their differences in parental philosophies, Mike and Lisa have been able to maintain a united front in the family. This has required compromise and patience, but the efforts have paid great dividends. For one thing, their girls weren't able to pit one parent against the other, thus dividing Mom and Dad and weakening the idea of the family as a team.

Be proactive and talk with your spouse about the boundaries you want to set before they become issues with your kids. Don't wait until they get older. Work out as many disagreements as you and your spouse may have before you need to implement any boundaries.

If unforeseen conflicts come up later, resolve them in private. Never argue in front of the kids. Make sure they hear you both saying the same thing. When parents are always disagreeing about what's best for their kids, their children begin to wonder if the family is in danger of falling apart. Your kids need to know you are together when it comes to family values and boundaries and consequences. When they do, they will feel secure, knowing that you love and respect each other. They will also be more likely to accept your boundaries without much resistance.

Agree on which few, well-chosen issues will not be open for discussion—period—and then stick to your word. Some parents falter in attempting to make every rule nonnegotiable; others falter in not having any nonnegotiables. Too many rules, and children will rebel; not enough rules, and children will rebel.

One of the nonnegotiable rules in our home is saying "please" and "thank you." I still remember waiting in the grocery store for fifteen minutes one day until one of my sons finally said "thank you" to the storekeeper who offered him a cookie.

If Mom and Dad are united on the nonnegotiables and enforce them when the kids are young, the teen years will go much smoother for all concerned. You'll be able to keep your cool under pressure because the decision has already been made. You can lower your voice to a whisper, even when your child is bellowing to negotiate.

Here's a case in point:

I didn't think much about it when the phone rang one Friday night, until it hit me that the boys were at a spend-the-night birthday party for a twelve-year-old. I reached for the receiver to hear, "Jill, I'm having a problem with your boys."

Like an army sergeant who just received word of an infraction with one of his men, I responded, "I'm on my way."

"Wait a minute . . . let me explain," Diane quickly said to stop the onslaught of the military. "We were getting ready to watch a movie, when the boys told me they weren't allowed to watch PG-13 movies."

My heart stopped pounding and swelled in my proud chest. "Oh, really? Well, that *is* true."

I told this mom the issue wasn't up for discussion, because one of our nonnegotiable house rules was no PG-13 movies until the boys were thirteen. So I offered to rent a couple of movies and bring them so the boys could watch a movie I deemed more appropriate. The mom agreed to put the birthday-party boys back in the backyard until I got there. If I had insisted the boys just come home, I would have thrown up a wall instead of preserving the boundary.

Was all that trouble worth it?

You'd better believe it!

Another way to ensure that boundaries don't become walls, in addition to having nonnegotiable boundaries both parents agree on, is to remember the importance of your relationship with your kids. When kids know they are loved and valued for who they are, they have a much easier time seeing boundaries as good things that are set up for their own protection.

Stay Emotionally Connected with Your Kids

IT'S IMPORTANT TO NOTE THAT when God gave Adam and Eve the boundary of not eating from the tree of the knowledge of good and evil, He was also "walking in the garden in the cool of the day"[4] with them. In other words, He spent time with them. He had a relationship with them. He wasn't simply dictating rules apart from His relationship with them.

I can think of no better way than this to ensure your boundaries don't become walls: spend time with your kids. Get involved in their world. For too long we've been told that children just need quality time, not quantity time. Not true. If you want to have an open and close relationship with your children, you must connect with them emotionally. I'm talking about a heart-to-heart connection. This can only happen when we're intimately involved in their lives.

> Children need **quantities** of quality time.
>
> —Wise Ol' Wilbur

Make sure your kids know you love them for who they are. If you try to establish firm boundaries outside the context of a close relationship with them, you will likely fail. But if you maintain closeness throughout their childhood, you'll pave the way for success. When we don't take time to develop and maintain a close relationship but still expect our rules to be followed, we erect walls.

Here are some ways to stay emotionally connected to your children throughout their growing-up years.

Tot and Tyke Years

IF YOU HAVE MORE THAN one child this age, go ahead and do these things with both of them. Kids this age don't yet need to spend individual time with you.

+ Have your kids lie next to you on the sofa for a back scratch following their afternoon playtime.

+ Have a regular downtime before supper.

+ Create a special good-night or good-morning ritual. For instance, the boys and I made up a wake-up song, which I sang to them every morning. My mother served us orange juice in bed on school mornings! (I didn't do this with my boys, but it's still a great idea.)

+ Eat meals together as a family.

+ Read books together at bedtime.

+ Read Bible stories and God's Word together every day.

+ When spending time together as a family, turn off the television and don't answer the phone. Protect your family time.

+ Play games together—catch, board games, hide-and-seek.

+ Color, do crafts, and make things together.

+ Cook or sew together.

Tween Years

KIDS THIS AGE NEED TO spend time with you alone, so if you have more than one child, do your best to give each of them that much-needed one-on-one time. Depending on their ages:

+ Go on regular lunch dates.

+ Volunteer as much as possible in school activities. Elementary-age children love having their parents at school. They swell with pride when *their* mom or dad walks in.

+ When talking with your children, make eye contact. Give them your focused attention.

+ Wash the car together.

+ Cook together—teach them how to bake a cake, make cookies, and cook simple meals.

+ Do crafts together . . . make a family scrapbook or a scrapbook about them.

+ Watch a movie together and then discuss it.

+ Be available for late-night talks.

+ Share spiritual lessons you're learning.

+ When appropriate, talk about your life and some of the mistakes you've made. They'll appreciate your vulnerability and love you for your imperfections.

Teen Years

AS KIDS GROW OLDER, IT often becomes more challenging to maintain a close relationship with them. Perhaps you have a teenager who is challenging your authority and whom you don't particularly enjoy being around. Pursue the relationship anyway. Spend time with her—just the two of you—and make sure she knows she is loved unconditionally.

Here are some additional ideas that can help you stay connected:

+ Use your cell phones to stay in touch throughout the day.

+ Send e-mails and e-cards that say, "I'm thinking of you."

+ Write your children a letter at least once a month.

+ Take a trip together.

+ Continue to share what God is doing in your life, opening the door for deep, meaningful talks.

Play fair.

Don't hit people.

Put things back where

you found them.

Clean up your own mess.

Don't take things

that aren't yours.

Say you're sorry when you

hurt somebody.

Take a nap every afternoon.

Flush.[5]

—Robert Fulghum,

*All I Really Need to Know
I Learned in Kindergarten*

Even when our kids leave home to go off to college or move into a place of their own, we still need to maintain a close relationship so they know they can come to us for guidance and support. Their world is rapidly changing, and it's important for parents to be available during the disappointments and moral issues that arise.

Again, if you maintain a united front and a close relationship with your children, you'll have a much easier time enforcing boundaries, no matter their ages.

Make Rules Age-Appropriate

YOUR BOUNDARIES WILL ALSO BE much less likely to create walls between you and your kids if you make your rules age-appropriate.

Tot and Tyke Years

DURING THEIR FIRST FIVE YEARS of life, one of your children's primary tasks is the development of the values that will influence them for the rest of their lives. That means you, the parent, have the opportunity to mold your child's character before the values of the disrespectful world have a chance to pull your child in the wrong direction.

One of the important values taught through boundary-setting is obedience. That's why I encourage parents to require "instant obedience." Those who allow their kids, even at this early age, to break the rules a few times before doling out consequences are setting themselves up for major battles later. Don't go there. Help your kids learn the value of obedience by following through with the consequence the first time the rule or boundary is broken.

When we set and enforce rules of behavior, we are not only protecting our children from harm and teaching them to be obedient, but we are also shaping their moral values and character. So, if you want your children to grow up to become respectful, honest, kind, and compassionate and to believe in the authority of God, you need to set boundaries that reflect those values. For example:

- ✦ Instill respect for others by establishing rules such as:

    1. No hitting or biting allowed.

    2. Use good manners. Say "please," "thank you," and "excuse me."

    3. Say "Have a good day" to employees at the grocery store, bank, and so on as you exit a business. (My mother insisted on this one. I did the same with my sons. The smiles that came from the recipients were enough to teach the value of showing respect to others.)

- ✦ Instill respect for self by establishing rules such as:

    1. Do not cross the street without an adult.

    2. Do not touch the stove when Mom is cooking.

3. No walking away from Mom or Dad in public places.

+ Teach the value of sharing by establishing rules such as:

1. Share your toys with your friends.

2. Keep one and share one when candy is given out.

3. Always let your friends go first.

Tween Years

SIX- TO TWELVE-YEAR-OLDS NEED TO be reminded of the rules and that there are consequences when they break them. When a boundary is broken, discipline swiftly, and clearly state the reason for the consequence. Put the burden on your children's shoulders—they can handle it. You want your children to experience the reality that *their* choices, not your choices, determine the discipline.

For example:

+ Teach the value of honesty by establishing rules such as:

1. Tell the truth, the whole truth, and nothing but the truth.

2. Do not blame others when you get in trouble. Take responsibility for your own actions.

3. Ask before using someone else's belongings.

✦ Instill a sense of responsibility by setting rules such as:

1. Use an alarm clock to wake up, dress, and be ready for school on time.

2. Complete homework before free time.

3. Be ready for bed by the established bedtime, without complaining.

✦ Teach the value of compassion by setting rules such as:

1. Feed and exercise your pet on the established schedule.

2. Don't play rough with younger siblings; use gentleness.

3. Apologize when you hurt someone's feelings.

Give your child privileges, such as being allowed to spend the night at a friend's house when he or she demonstrates maturity in accepting your house rules.

The Year In Between

FOR MANY YEARS I GAVE a lecture each September to a group of new sixth-grade parents, breaking the news as gently as possible of the traumatic change that will take place in the life of their child during the upcoming school year. Children begin sixth grade agreeing with their parents' belief system. But by the end of the school year, the world begins to play a more prominent role in forming who the children become.

During this year children begin forming their own opinions, making decisions about what they believe. They no longer blindly accept their parents' views, but begin to decide for themselves what is right and wrong. What they decide will be influenced by the discrepancies they see in adults' thinking and actions. By the end of their sixth-grade year, your kids will have become their own persons, either accepting or rejecting your views according to the authenticity they've seen in your life.

I know we've talked about the importance of your example, but it is particularly critical when your kids are in this in-between year. If you want them to "own" your values, they must see that you live by your word. They must see you living within the boundaries you have set for them, just as you expect your kids to live within those boundaries.

Early Teen Years (ages thirteen to sixteen)

DURING THIS STAGE, SOME PARENTS back off and allow their kids more freedom than those kids are ready to handle. This is often in response to their children's moving toward independence from their parents. Yet the teen years are not the time to turn our backs. Instead, we should double our efforts to keep the relationship strong, the communication channels open, and the "rules of the house" in place.

For example:

✦ Teach the value of honesty by expecting your teens to:

1. Ask permission before borrowing someone else's belongings

2. Always tell the truth

3. Do what they say they are going to do

✦ Teach the value of purity by expecting your teens to:

1. Not view R-rated movies or play violent video games

2. Not use coarse language or name-call

3. Not spend time alone with the opposite sex

✦ Teach the value of self-respect by expecting your teens to:

1. Attend weekly church services

2. Dress modestly

3. Resist peer pressure

Late Teen Years (ages seventeen to nineteen)

YOUR TEEN BELIEVES HE IS now an adult. So treat him like one. Give more responsibility and more privileges accordingly. Insist on adherence to the established rules. With a strong relationship already in place, the later teen years can be a wonderful time for you and your children. They're still under your authority, but moving from dependence to interdependence.

Don't be fooled into believing there should no longer be boundaries. Boundaries are just as important at this stage as at any other. In some ways they are even more important, because this is your last opportunity to instill your values before your teens enter adulthood.

For example:

✦ Teach the value of self-discipline by expecting your young adults to:

>   1. Be punctual

>   2. Practice good study habits

✦ Instill the value of money by requiring your young adults to:

>   1. Get a summer job during high school and college

>   2. Pay for their clothes, cell phones, dining out, and entertainment

✦ Instill a sense of responsibility by requiring your young adults to:

>   1. Do their own laundry

>   2. Take care of their own cars

>   3. Help prepare family meals

Keep in mind that your boundaries serve to help protect your children until they are mature enough to establish their own boundaries.

Good Boundaries Build Respectful Adults

SHORTLY BEFORE HE RETURNED TO the Father, Jesus said to His disciples, "I no longer call you servants, because a servant does not know his master's business. Instead, I have called you friends, for everything that I learned from my Father I have made known to you."[6] Jesus' words deeply reflected His love for the disciples and His desire to equip them with everything they needed for their lives to be fruitful, even after He was no longer with them.

Someday we will call our sons and daughters "friend," and they will feel the same about us. While we don't stop being a parent, we will gradually move from a "parent/child relationship" to an "adult/ adult relationship." Wise parents proactively plan for that day, because they know it will come sooner than they think.

Start planning today how you can use age-appropriate boundaries to help your children achieve the maturity required to successfully handle the freedoms and responsibilities of adulthood.

7

Use Discipline, Not Punishment

HAVE YOU EVER heard of a "predictable surprise"? Max Bazerman and Michael Watkins, faculty at the Harvard Business School, coined the term "predictable surprise" and define it as "an event or set of events that take an individual or group by surprise, despite prior awareness of all of the information necessary to anticipate the events and their consequences."[1]

Predictable surprises are problems that some people are aware of, but not addressing fast enough to prevent severe damage. Over time, the problems get worse, and sooner or later they are likely to explode into a crisis.

The levee surrounding New Orleans proved to be a "predictable surprise." Many had warned of the potential for collapse in the event of a strong storm, but no one heeded the warning. No one was willing to admit that there needed to be changes made. The problems behind a "predictable surprise" always require a significant investment in the near term that will not pay off until later. In other words, time and effort must be expended in the short term to avoid problems in the long term.

The discipline of children works that way. Unless time and effort are invested in your children when they're young, you'll have a "predictable surprise" on your hands by the time they become teens. I like to call it "preventive parenting." You can ward off future problems by stopping them before they have a chance to start.

In this chapter, we'll discuss the most effective method of preventive parenting—discipline that brings respect, rather than punishment that brings resentment. As Scripture tells us, "No discipline seems pleasant at the time, but painful. Later on, however, it produces a harvest of righteousness and peace for those who have been trained by it."[2] I hope you'll make the decision to live with unpleasantness from time to time in the short term, to yield years of great peace in the long term.

Consider yourself forewarned. I don't want you to be surprised one day by a teen who implodes from lack of discipline or who crumbles under the weight of punishment.

*   *   *

A FATHER BATTLING HIS SEVENTEEN-YEAR-OLD son's lack of respect had reached the end of his rope. With great pride, he told me about his solution to a scene that had occurred a few days earlier: "I was sick and tired of his lack of motivation. His attitude. He has never listened to me, not even when he was a little kid. He's never been interested in anything I wanted him to do with me. And that music. Have you heard that garbage? The only words I understood were the ones I use when I hope nobody's listening—and his friends were getting stranger every day.

"The final straw came last weekend. He stole two bottles of whiskey from my liquor cabinet for a party with his buddies. When I caught him red-handed, all he said was, 'You drink, Dad, and so what's the big deal?' Okay, so I drink a few after work, but I'm an adult and he's a kid. I told him I wouldn't put up with his disrespect and excuses any longer. Told him enough was enough. He said he'd rather live on the street than in the house with me. So, I kicked him out. Told him to figure out life on his own. Maybe now he'll learn something."

When I asked this father how long he had been disappointed in his son's behavior, he replied, "Since the day he was born. He's just a bad apple."

A *bad apple*—from birth? What about the adage "The apple doesn't fall far from the tree"? Could that be the case with this father and son? Every child has a soul that needs to be nourished and a heart that needs to be protected. Just as a seed planted in the ground is dependent on the gardener to survive, so is a child totally dependent on a parent to thrive emotionally. How much time had this father spent in the garden of his son's heart? This father needs to understand that he is reaping the fruit from the seeds *he* planted.

Children need love, and they also need discipline. Parents who love their children will lovingly discipline them. By his own account, this father had not given his son the love and discipline all children need to grow up to become respectful adults.

Discipline Leads to Respect

THE LACK OF DISCIPLINE IN a home is just as much a sign of neglect as not providing food and shelter. Just as every child needs to know someone loves her unconditionally and, no matter what, someone will be there for her, every child also needs to know there are limits to acceptable behavior.

Discipline comes from the Latin root *discipere*, which means "to grasp intellectually, analyze thoroughly," from *dis*—"apart" + *capere*—"take." When parents discipline their kids, they are taking apart a problem in order to thoroughly analyze it. Discipline is meant to prevent future problems, not just solve immediate problems. It teaches, instructs, and trains. *Webster's* defines discipline as "training that corrects, molds, or perfects the mental faculties or moral character."[3] For example:

+ Your two-year-old pushes her milk off the table.

  Discipline: She helps you clean it up.

  Lesson learned: We are all responsible for our own messes.

+ Your ten-year-old has "forgotten" to take out the trash two weeks in a row.

  Discipline: For the next two weeks, he has to do the additional chore of helping with supper.

  Lesson learned: Better to do the chores we're assigned than to neglect them. When we neglect our responsibilities, it only makes the situation worse.

Discipline is more about teaching our children what to do than about teaching them what not to do. When we discipline them, we show them the better way. Our discipline enables them to become better tomorrow than they are today. To grow. To mature. To become responsible, respectful members of society. Discipline teaches kids to *do* good rather than *feel* good.

> **Discipline** is teaching kids to do good rather than feel good.
> —Wise Ol' Wilbur

Discipline changes an undesirable behavior, teaches a life lesson, or persuades children to think before they make a decision. It helps them become all they are intended to be.

Punishment, however, crushes children.

Punishment Leads to Rebellion

DISCIPLINE AND PUNISHMENT ARE NOT the same thing. *Punishment* can be defined as "retributive suffering, pain or loss; rough treatment."[4] That's a far cry from the meaning of *discipline*, which is action that "corrects, molds, or perfects the mental faculties or moral character." Punishment belittles; it doesn't motivate.

For example:

+ A thirteen-year-old makes a sarcastic remark to her mom in front of a store clerk. The mom responds, "You will not embarrass me like that in public."

    Punishment: The mom makes her daughter walk behind her down the mall and out to the parked car.

    Lesson learned: My mom humiliates me. Why shouldn't I humiliate her?

+ Later that day, the teen doesn't come in time to help her mom put supper on the table.

    Punishment: Mom sends the daughter to her room for the night with the words, "If you're not going to help me, I don't want to see your face."

    Lesson learned: My mom doesn't care about me; she just expects me to make her life easier. Why should I, when she makes my life harder?

Unfortunately, the above examples really happened, and when I tried to talk to this mom about the situation with her daughter, she told me, "She is my child, and I expect her to treat me with respect. It's not about her; it's about me."

I'm afraid the handwriting is on the wall in this home. This daughter's willful disobedience is a response to her mom's inappropriate and unloving punishment.

By the age of fifteen, this girl was in full-blown rebellion, doing anything she could to publicly embarrass her mom. She's now twenty years old and beginning to understand that it's not only her mom she has been embarrassing, but herself. How sad that her teen years have been such a struggle! Mother and daughter are both learning life lessons the hard way.

The harder parents try to demand respect from their children through punishment, the more resentment builds, which causes rebellion.

We can't demand respect from our kids; we must command it. Respect is earned. Your children will respect you if you are working on their behalf to help them reach their full potential. They'll even accept tough penalties more readily, if your motive is right. If your attempts at discipline aren't working, chances are, you're using punishment, not discipline. You are seeking to satisfy yourself, not train your child.

I have known parents who are mystified when their teen rebels, even though the parents were tough disciplinarians. They say things like: "I didn't let my kid get away with disrespect." "I insisted my kid tow the line." "My daughter wasn't allowed to act unladylike." But what was the motive behind these parents' toughness? I'm sure they told their children what to do, but did they train their kids through effective discipline—or did they punish them? I suspect it was the latter. Punishment for the sole purpose of forcing compliance will be ineffective. When the rules are about maintaining control rather than helping the child learn important life lessons, the child finds little respect for the rules or the rule-maker.

Compare the differences between discipline and punishment in the following chart.

DISCIPLINE	vs.	PUNISHMENT
Leads to change		Leads to little change
Encourages		Discourages
Educates (teaches right from wrong)		Shames
For the child's benefit		For the parent's benefit
Comes from love		Comes from fear
Encourages respect		Encourages resentment
Leads to self-discipline		Leads to rebellion

Scripture tells us, "Do not exasperate your children; *instead*, bring them up in the training and instruction of the Lord."[5] In other words, use discipline, not punishment. If you punish your kids, you will exasperate (irritate, aggravate, enrage) them. Your children know your motives, even when you don't. If you want to know what your motive is . . . ask your kids; they can tell you. They see things as they are, not as we want them to be. Children know whether your discipline is about you or them.

Which do you choose, discipline or punishment? Respect or resentment? If your goal is to raise respectful children, I urge you to try discipline and leave punishment behind. Ultimately, the goal of discipline is to help your children develop self-discipline—to be capable of policing themselves—so your penalties are no longer necessary.

As I've quoted before: "No discipline seems pleasant at the time, but painful. Later on, however, it produces a harvest of righteousness and peace for those who have been trained by it."[6] It couldn't be any clearer than that! Discipline isn't easy; it's even painful in the short term, but it leads to respectfulness.

Preventive Discipline

THE SUMMER BETWEEN ELEVENTH AND twelfth grades, my sons decided to pull their first "stunt." When I called the home of a friend
where they'd said they were staying on a Saturday morning to remind them of an early obligation, I discovered they weren't there and
had not been, all night.

I spent nearly three hours on the phone, searching for the boys.
When they finally drove up the driveway around noon, I was too
angry to even speak. They had spent the night at a forbidden home
with no parents present. Up until then, their infractions of my rules
had been misdemeanors. I considered this particular infraction a
major crime that warranted major sentencing. It took two weeks for
me to settle on an appropriate penalty, during which time my boys
treated me like a queen rather than a judge. "Mom, can I help you
with supper tonight?" "Mom, I thought I'd wash your car, just because . . ."

When the day of sentencing came, Judge Jill convened Court
Rigby in the hallowed halls of our kitchen. "The privilege you abused
was spending the night out," I began. "You decided you had a right to
spend the night wherever you chose. You were wrong. You no longer
have the privilege of spending the night at a friend's house. Is that
understood?"

After a bit of stunned silence, Chad spoke up. "Can we go out
for a couple of hours at night?"

"You can go out at night, but you are not allowed to spend the
night out. That privilege has been lost . . . that's it. Court dismissed,"
I said as I pounded the rubber mallet on the cutting board.

All was well until school began in the fall. Chad called right
after the season's first football game to say, "Mom, we're going to
spend the night at Matt's."

"No, I don't think so," I replied.

"Why not, Mom?" Chad questioned.

Swallowing hard before speaking again, I said, "You lost that privilege."

"But that was just for the summer," he retorted.

"No, the sentence was handed down without a time stipulation," I explained. "Sorry, I'll see you both at home in twenty minutes."

I hung up the phone, terrified that rebellion had arrived. I was hoping the boys would drive up, but frankly, I didn't really believe they would.

I was wrong. Twenty-two minutes later, Chad and Boyce walked past me in the kitchen without a word. They just looked in my eyes and nodded affirmatively.

The issue was settled.

I know you're wondering why my sons accepted this stiff discipline with such grace. After all, they were seniors in high school! I can tell you, it had very little to do with the tone of my voice or their fear of future consequences. It goes back to what we talked about in Chapter 3, "Enroll in the School of Respect." The reason my sons didn't rebel against my discipline that night was all their years in the School of Respect, being raised with preventive discipline. My sons trusted me, and they knew I loved them unconditionally. They also recognized the decision to violate my trust came with a consequence, and they knew from experience that I would follow through.

Please don't misunderstand. I'm not saying my boys obeyed me because I was the perfect parent. I wasn't. I made plenty of mistakes, such as the time I forgot to pick them up from soccer practice or the day I lost my cool and chewed them out only to discover they had done nothing wrong. And there were plenty of instances when I said yes but should have said no.

But the boys understood that when I said no, the matter was not open for discussion. I tried my best to make decisions for my own life that reflected my belief system. If I expected the boys to be ready on time for school, I had to be punctual too. If I expected the boys to clean up after themselves, I had to keep the house picked up too. Most of all I tried to make discipline decisions with the big picture in mind, always asking myself, *Who do I want the boys to become?* I was concerned about their character. My aim was to help them learn to respect others, to respect rules, and to respect themselves.

My sons recognized:

+ The certainty of my unconditional *love*

+ The fair *consequence* for their disobedience to our house rule was deserved

+ I would follow through on the penalty, and there was no need for further discussion

If we're doing our job as parents, our kids must know that our discipline comes from our love for them and our desire to help them become respectful, responsible adults. To achieve that end, we must administer consequences that reinforce the lessons we're teaching.

In other words, preventive discipline must be a combination of love, consequences, and follow-through. Let's take a closer look at how we can effectively implement these methods.

Discipline from a Heart of Love

PAUL TELLS US "THE GOAL of our instruction [discipline] is love from a pure heart and a good conscience and a sincere faith."[7] This scripture can serve as our guide to ensure that our discipline is motivated by a heart of love for our child.

From a Pure Heart

PREPARE YOUR HEART BEFORE THE need for discipline arises by using Psalm 139 as a daily prayer: "Search me, O God, and know my heart; test me and know my anxious thoughts. See if there is an *offensive* way in me, and lead me in the way everlasting."[8] This exercise will reveal the good and the bad that resides in your heart, better preparing you to use discipline rather than punishment.

From a Good Conscience

SAY WHAT YOU MEAN, AND mean what you say. The fastest way to fail at discipline is to not carry through on the demands you've made, so be careful not to say things you don't really mean:

- ✦ "If you don't clean your room, you won't be allowed to eat for a month."

- ✦ "Timmy, if I have to ask you one more time to not slam the door, I'll lock you out for good."

Your kids will take you at your word. You can't backtrack or expect them to second-guess you. You can't say, "Well, what I meant to say was . . ." We need to do our best to get it right the first time.

From a Sincere Faith

LET YOUR CHILDREN KNOW YOU are not the final authority, but that you answer to God and His principles. Your kids will be much more willing to come under your authority when they understand that you come under God's authority.

I mentioned early on that the experts have changed their minds countless times in the past two hundred years on the proper way to raise children. However, Scripture hasn't changed—not one word. Truth doesn't have to change with the whims of society. It stands the test of time.

> Any child can be taught to be **beautifully** behaved with no effort greater than quiet patience and perseverance, whereas to break bad habits once they are acquired is a Herculean task.
> —Emily Post (1872–1960)

For your discipline to be effective, your kids should not only know that you love them and want the best for them; they must also know that with disobedience comes consequences.

Discipline through Consequences

OF THE MANY CONSEQUENCES THAT might come to mind, I think the following are most effective:

Distraction, Time-Out, and Loss of Privileges

INFANTS NEED PROTECTION AS THEY explore the world around them. We can train babies and toddlers to avoid danger by diverting their attention when they "misbehave." A toddler's attention span is short, so the dangerous activity is quickly forgotten. If distraction doesn't work, physically move your child away from the trouble. For example, if your child continues exploring a light socket when asked to stop, pick him up and move him to another room for several minutes.

When your child is between the ages of three and six, use timeout as a consequence for misbehavior. Tell your child, "You didn't

follow the rule, so you'll have to sit out until you're ready to obey."
This consequence reminds me of the children's game "Simon Says."
We all know the
rules . . . you are
allowed to move
only when Simon
says. If you move
before he says to
move, you're out of
the game. If your
tyke disobeys a rule,
he has to sit out for

Spanking

I believe if all else fails, as a last resort,
spanking can be an appropriate option
with children from age two to six who are
outright defiant or in danger.

a while. Use a kitchen timer set at three minutes for this age group.
If your child gets up before the timer goes off, reset it, without
discussion, and start over. Your child will finally give in, if you don't
give up.

Time-out for tweens and teens comes in the form of the loss of
privileges as a consequence of disobedience. Give an instruction
once; if not followed, follow through by taking away a privilege. If
your tween breaks a house rule about TV watching, take away all
TV privileges for two days. As your tween grows, extend the time
that the privilege is removed. For example, if your twelve-year-old
daughter breaks a rule about the telephone, tell her she won't be able
to use the telephone for a week. If your sixteen-year-old abuses her
cell-phone privileges, she loses the phone for one month (one billing
cycle!).

Natural Consequences

PAINFUL AS IT MAY BE for both of you, children must accept the consequences of their own decisions. It's tempting to rescue them, but
the best discipline is self-discipline. It's through mistakes that the

greatest lessons are learned. Stepping in to "fix things" will hinder, not help, the maturation process. Let your child face the consequences of poor choices.

Chad was a forgetful fourth grader until the day he found out he would have to count on his own mind rather than his mom's servant heart to remember his schoolwork. I made the round trip from home to school to home and back to school two days in one week to help Chad cover his forgetfulness.

The following Monday morning it happened again, even after reminding the boys to check their backpacks for all needed schoolwork. Just as Chad jumped out of the car, he remembered the papers he'd left on his desk.

Public Humiliation

Recently there's been a storm of incidents where a parent puts her child on a street corner with a sandwich board sign that tells of the child's offense. Much of the public seems to applaud the parents for getting tough with unruly teenagers.

I disagree.

Serious willful disobedience does not happen overnight. If the parent was driven to such drastic measures, there must be something missing behind the scenes. I would rather see the parents stand on the street corner with a sign confessing their failure to parent during the teenager's younger years.

Public humiliation should never be an option. Instead, deal with issues as they arise so that you never feel compelled to resort to such damaging measures.

"Mom, will you pleeeeeeeeeeeease go get my math sheet? I don't have class until ten o'clock. Thank you, Mom," he said with all the confidence in the world of my servitude. But this time I responded with a statement he had not heard before: "No, Chad, I won't do that today." It was apparent that he had not learned his lesson, but I had learned mine. It was time for Chad to suffer the consequences of his forgetfulness.

You would have thought by his reaction that I had told him to kiss his brother! His nine-year-old tantrum rivaled the most horrific two-year-old tantrum I had ever seen. And of course, it took place in the carpool line in front of other moms dropping off their angels. After being told to move out of the line and watching my child being pulled away from the car by an understanding teacher, I drove away with tears puddling in my lap. I circled the block wanting to return to school to ask my son to forgive me, but I knew in my heart that I was doing the best thing for Chad, even though he would receive a zero on his assignment.

When I returned for the afternoon pickup, Chad had obviously surmised that his best course of action was to be quiet and nonconfrontational with his mom. Finally we "kissed and made up" at supper. No apology for my decision, but a big hug with "I love you." "Yeah, I know," was Chad's reply.

You already know without my saying it, he was never forgetful again.

I have a dear friend, an English professor, who reports that more and more parents are calling to discuss their college student's grades. She is appalled at the audacity of the parents and also saddened, because it seems to be the students needing the most "growing up" whose parents are the ones calling her. "Counterproductive," in her words.

Repetition

THIS IS THE MOST EFFECTIVE consequence I know. It can be used no matter the age of your child—and it's almost fun! Sound too good to be true? Read on.

One night, six-year-old Boyce put the last bit of macaroni and cheese in his mouth at the supper table. He jumped up from the table and headed to his room to finish his latest Lego creation.

"Now, wait a minute. Didn't you forget something?" I said just before he reached the doorway. "Remember what we do before we leave the table? Back up and give me ten."

Stomping his foot, he replied, "Aw, Mom."

Too much **talk** and you'll talk yourself into trouble and your child out of trouble.

—Wise Ol' Wilbur

With a scowl across his face, he returned to the table to finish his supper the proper way. Holding his dinner plate, he asked, "May I be excused, please?"

I replied, "Yes, you may."

He stood with dish in hand, walked to the sink, and placed it in the basin. Sighing, he reached in, picked it up again, and returned to the table and sat down.

He began again, "May I please be . . ."

Again, I replied, "Yes, you may."

The third time Boyce did this, his dad, brother, and I began to giggle. Soon Boyce's scowl became a sheepish grin as he broke into boisterous laughter.

By the tenth repetition, I could barely stammer, "Yes, you may." The whole family was in stitches.

How many times do you think I had to remind Boyce to say, "May I be excused, please" after that night? You're right, never again. Chad, on the other hand, had to learn this lesson for himself two weeks later. A grand reminder to me that all children, even identical twins, are unique individuals with their own time-tables.

Yes, it takes time and patience to use repetition as a consequence, but as you can see, this is an effective way to discipline and can be fun too. *Remember, the goal of discipline is not to punish, but to change a behavior pattern.*

Not only is repetition an effective way to correct bad manners, it can also be used to curb the use of inappropriate or bad language. If your child uses an inappropriate word, ask her to say the sentence ten times, replacing the inappropriate word with a silly word, such as *popcorn*, *peanut butter*, or *stinks*. For example, if she says, "That's just stupid," have her repeat, "That's just popcorn" ten times. Next time she'll be less likely to use the word *stupid*.

Repetition for foul language also works on teens, but in addition to giving a silly word, I recommend giving them an appropriate alternative. For instance, if your son says something "sucks," you can ask him to say *stinks* twenty-two times. I even used *supercalifragilisticexpialidocious* on one occasion for a particularly foul word—and I requested thirty-two repetitions!

Perhaps you're thinking, *I don't have time to fool with this nonsense. Waiting for my child to repeat something thirty-two times . . .*

I beg to differ.

Disciplining through repetition will save you time, energy, and heartache in the long run. If you are willing to stand by the "give me ten" rule with gentle firmness, you can motivate your kids to change an unwanted behavior in only a few attempts. It's rare that a parent has to repeat the same exercise more than three times in order to help a child change a bad habit or instill a good one.

Why does repetition lead to behavior change? I can think of two reasons:

1. *You're offering an alternative to the wrong behavior and reinforcing it.* When you give a substitute to replace the unwanted behavior, you're training, not just doling out a penalty.

2. *It takes the sting out of the discipline.* Even the child being corrected becomes amused at the silliness of the repetition, but since our goal is to change an unwanted behavior or instill a good one, who says

the discipline always has to be miserable? There are times when doing whatever it takes to help your child change is fun! And your child is motivated to change when the discipline focuses on the behavior instead of on him.

But so often in our hurriedness and exhaustion, we let our guards down and don't complete our mission of preventive discipline. Love and consequences will produce change only when we follow through.

Always Follow Through

A FEW FINAL POINTS TO ponder about follow-through, no matter the age of your child:

+ *United you stand; divided you fall.* As was pointed out in the previous chapter, you and your spouse are co-coaches on the home team. If two coaches on the same team gave you opposing orders, the team would be defeated. If you disagree with each other, do so in private. Your children will use you against each other if you're not careful to maintain a united front.

+ *Be consistent.* Don't change your mind with the wind. When you're tempted to give in or tempted to bend the rules, remember that you're the parent.

+ *Take action.* Go over the offense and give the consequence, and then move on. We complicate issues of discipline by discussing and explaining. Do you really expect your child to look at you after being disciplined and say, "Oh, I understand, Dad. I get it now; you've just taken away my CD player because you love me and . . ."? Chances of that happening at that moment are slim to none.

✦ *Use your child's name, no matter the age.* "Jonathan, I'd like you to take out the garbage." By using your child's name, you're conveying the child's personal responsibility for the requested action. It also helps to develop his pride in a job well done. Your child is thinking, Dad called me by name . . . I'd better listen.

✦ *Decide ahead of time that you will win.* You're not battling your child; you're battling the wrongness of your child's behavior. For the sake of your child, you must win.

✦ *Stay calm.* Let a young child know by your calm demeanor that whining is absolutely, positively ineffective. You can nip whining in the bud by ignoring it. If a teen whines, explain the reason for your decision to say no, and stand by it. You can discuss alternatives, but not compromises.

> **Discipline** is the bridge between goals and accomplishments.
> —Jim Rohn

✦ *Don't be hesitant.* Your child can hear it in your voice. Use a firm voice with confidence.

✦ *Expect the best.* Your children will live up to your expectations if your heart is in the right place.

✦ *Just say no.* When the answer needs to be no, just say so. No need to belabor an explanation. Be firm but loving, confident but kind. Then let it go and move on.

✦ *Offer a statement, not a question.* Rather than "Would you like to go clean up your room now?" simply say, "Sally, it's time to clean your room." If you ask a question, you're giving your child the option to decide whether to obey or not.

✦ *Do not repeat yourself.* You want to teach your child to respond to your request the first time. If your child discovers that you'll ask repeatedly, he'll ignore you until you lose your cool, because you've programmed him to think there's more than one chance to obey.

✦ *Lower your voice.* When your child raises her voice, lower yours. The louder she gets, the quieter you must be. Your child will hear what you're saying, even if you think she's not listening. She wants to know what you're saying. If you're whispering, she has to calm down to hear you.

✦ *Never use "don't."* I believe there must be a switch at the base of a child's neck that reacts to the word don't. It's like having a remote control in your hand. When you say, "How many times have I told you, don't run in the house," and your child looks at you as if he's never heard you say that, believe it. He really hasn't heard you. Instead, say, "You're not allowed to run in the house. Stop in your tracks, and sit down for a while."

✦ *Fit the discipline to the crime.* An annoying child needs to be alone until she decides to no longer be annoying but to be helpful to others. If a child hits another child, tell her to hug that child ten times. If she leaves the yard, she loses the privilege of playing in the yard and must stay inside for the rest of the day.

✦ *When you do make mistakes, ask your child's forgiveness.*
The level of respect your child has for you skyrockets
when you're willing to humble yourself and ask for his
forgiveness when you've been wrong. And following
your example, your child will do the same for you.

✦ *Be a parent first, a friend second.* During your children's
teen years your relationship with them is changing from
parent to friend, but you are still the parent, and teens
need a parent more than another friend.

Parents who parent with a character-centered perspective use
preventive discipline to meet their end goal—raising a respectful, responsible adult who is actively pursuing his or her purpose. Your
children can move from your governance to self-governance if along
the way you have given them ample opportunities to make their own
decisions and receive the benefits of good decisions, while suffering
the consequences of bad ones.

Your reward is a close relationship with your children based on
mutual trust and respect. Your child's reward is self-respect.

The Reward

EFFECTIVE PREVENTIVE DISCIPLINE DEVELOPS SELF-DISCIPLINE in
your child—the ability and desire to do the right thing because it's
the right thing to do. Through instruction and discipline of moral
character, your child develops respect for God, others, and self. The
child who masters self-discipline is a child with self-respect who will
go on to become all that you could ever hope or envision.

As wise King Solomon once said, "The corrections of discipline
are the way of life."[9]

8

Shield Your Treasures from the Trash:

Magazines, Books, and Music

IN THE MID-SIXTIES, legislation was passed authorizing a hurricane protection project, which included a levee system around New Orleans that would protect the city from category 3 storms, which were expected every two hundred to three hundred years.[1]

Less than fifty years later, a category 4 storm hit. But it wasn't the storm that decimated New Orleans; it was the "predictable surprise," the failure of the levees that allowed raging Mississippi River waters through, flooding 80 percent of the city. Much has been written about the reasons for the breakdown of the levees. Some believed the footings were not deep enough in many places, only six to ten feet rather than twenty feet. Others believed the materials used were substandard. Still others believed the original design was flawed.

In the final assessment, everyone was right to some degree. The protection project underestimated the threat of flooding from larger storms. Local, state, and federal officials had been well aware of the vulnerability of the levees for many years. Voices of concern were raised from time to time by citizens who recognized breaches in the walls, but as so often happens, no one did anything to address the issue. The day came when it was too late to keep the walls from tumbling down.

Just as the storm surge pushed the levee until it gave way, the unending blows from the producers of books, magazines, and music are eroding the moral fiber of our society. The protective walls of respect and responsibility that once upheld a standard of decency have been pierced with images and words no one should see or hear, much less children. Pictures once reserved for behind-the-counter magazines now grace the pages of magazines for teenage girls. Required summer reading lists now include books filled with profanity, sex, and violence. Music videos no longer teach a new dance step but a new way of satisfying a sexual appetite. Nothing is taboo.

Decades ago, parents could raise their children with the assurance of support from the cultural norms. Today, parents must raise their children in opposition to the cultural norms. No wonder we're weary; we're trying to hold the walls in place all by ourselves.

In this chapter, we will take a closer look at the inundation of filth from the print world. We will discuss the sources of the deluge and ways to keep the filth from overtaking your children. And you'll learn ways you can push back the disrespectful sources.

We must do more than protect our children. We must protect *all* children. Together, we can build a mighty force for good.

✳ ✳ ✳

"FATHER, WHAT IS SEX SIN?" young Corrie ten Boom asked her father during a train ride as they returned home from a business trip to the city. She relates the story in her autobiography, *The Hiding Place*:

My father turned to look at me, as he always did when answering a question, but to my surprise he said nothing. At last he stood up, lifted his traveling case from the rack over our heads, and set it on the floor. "Will you carry it off the train, Corrie?" he said. I stood up and tugged at it. It was crammed with the watches and spare parts he had purchased that morning. "It's too heavy," I said. "Yes," he said. "And it would be a pretty poor father who would ask his little girl to carry such a load. It's the same way, Corrie, with knowledge. Some knowledge is too heavy for children. When you are older and stronger you can bear it. For now you must trust me to carry it for you."[2]

How do we shield our children, our precious treasures, from the trash in a culture that bombards them with immorality at every turn? Corrie ten Boom's father had the right answer—we, as parents, must bear the burden for them. We must shield their eyes and hearts from hurtful images and wrong messages.

To protect your treasures from the trash, you must be aware of what your children are seeing and hearing. You can't protect them if you don't know they are in danger. I'm afraid your kids already know more than you think, so you need to know even more . . .

Do you know what's out there? Read on and you will. In this chapter we will look at how our kids are being exposed to disrespectful messages and images in magazines, books, and music, and what you can do to protect your kids from these messages. In the next chapter we'll do the same with movies, TV, video games, and the Internet.

Disrespectful Messages in Magazines

I RECENTLY STOOD IN A sea of magazines at a national bookstore chain. My eyes jumped from sexual images to sexual innuendoes and back again, making me seasick. What used to be seen only inside pornographic magazines is now blatantly displayed on the covers of mainstream publications.

Don't be mistaken—I'm not talking about magazines targeted for adult readership. Magazine moguls target girls as young as ten with periodicals that contain adult content.[3] I assure you, twelve-year-old girls know all the "hot mags." Yes, even your own daughters.

Soft porn is rampant in teen magazines—*Cosmo Girl, Elle Girl, Young Miss,* and *Teen Vogue,* just to name a few. And that's not the only problem. The publishers of these magazines know if they can lure a ten-year-old into reading *Cosmo Girl,* she'll be reading *Cosmopolitan* by her thirteenth birthday.

Much discussion has ensued through the years that *Cosmopolitan* is much more than soft porn. In 2011, Victoria Hearst, an heir to the Hearst publishing empire that publishes *Cosmo,* joined forces with former model Nicole Weider on a campaign to put the sexually explicit magazine in a wrapper and ensure that it is sold only to those over the age of eighteen.[4] (My hope is that by the time of this printing, these two ladies will have accomplished their mission.)

It's not only the images in these magazines that are destructive; it's the articles, too, many of which aren't even appropriate for adults. For example:

"Sex Special"

"Hot Tips, Toys, and More"

"How to Score Like You're on Vacation Every Day"

"Your Hot Summer Sex and Love"

"Tips That Will Make You Feel Like a Goddess in 60 Seconds"

"Sex Talk"

"10 Sex Sins Thou Shalt Not Commit Tonight"

"Ditch the Rules and Release Your Inner Sinner!"

"His Secret Sex Craving"

"I Stole My Best Friend's Boyfriend"

"Find His Dominant Sense and Send Him into Orbit"

"Make Over Your Body"

"Seven Moves to a Strong and Sexy Body"

Don't think boys are any less impressionable than girls when it comes to the magazines. When exposed to sexual images, their respect for the opposite sex diminishes greatly, because the message being communicated is that girls are objects of men's pleasure.

The magazines are troubling, but books often morph into something much bigger.

Disrespectful Messages in Books

I CO-HOST A HALF-HOUR RADIO broadcast, *Reality Check*, in which we discuss current trends that threaten our children. On a broadcast in 2006 we highlighted a series of books for tween girls called the *Gossip Girl* series. The first book, *Gossip Girl*, opened with these words:

Ever wondered what the lives of the chosen ones are really like? Well, I'm going to tell you, because I'm one of them. . . .

I'm talking about the people who are *born to it*—those of us who have everything anyone could possibly wish for and who take it all completely for granted.

Welcome to New York City's Upper East Side, where my friends and I live and go to school and play and sleep—sometimes with each other. . . . We have unlimited access to money and booze and whatever else we want, and our parents are rarely home, so we have tons of privacy. We're smart, we've inherited classic good looks, we wear fantastic clothes, and we know how to party. Our ___ still stinks, but you can't smell it because the bathroom is sprayed hourly by the maid with a refreshing scent made exclusively for us by French perfumers.[5]

Forgive me for exposing you to this, but your daughters are reading it. The books in this series continue to fill the slots on the *New York Times* Children's Books bestseller list. (Yes, *children's* bestseller list.) Upon its publication, book number eight took the number-one slot. In May 2008, a follow-up series, *Gossip Girl: The Carlyles*, began publication, following the Carlyle triplets as they begin moving to the Upper East Side. As of October 2009, four novels had been released in this series. The series' author, Cecily von Ziegesar, created a spin-off series, *The It Girl*, which began publication in 2005, and Yen Press has adapted the series into a manga (comic book) series titled *Gossip Girl: For Your Eyes Only*.

The book series had sold 2.2 million copies by 2006. Today, more than 6 million copies have flown off the shelves into the hands of tweens and young teens. This is frightening, considering the kinds of disrespectful messages these books are broadcasting to young girls with impressionable minds:

✦ Lesbian sex is cool.

+ Value is in your status, not your character.

+ There are no boundaries.

+ Promiscuity is acceptable.

+ With enough money you can get away with anything,
  and if you don't have enough money, you can pretend.

The most disrespectful message of *Gossip Girls* is best explained in "15 Going On 50: How Gossip Girl Is Killing Youth Culture," in which Lesley Blume writes:

> *Gossip Girl* seems to tell us that there's nothing to look forward to, and there will be nothing to look back upon . . . except more of the same. We're not just destined to become brittle materialistic adults; we already *are* brittle materialistic adults by the time we hit puberty. We have no choice. We're wired for misery. If we have money, we're destined to be miserable with it. If we don't have it, we're destined to be miserable without it, and spend our lives with our noses pressed up against the glass. And this demoralizing little message is the *real* meanness of the series.[6]

A group of readers from ages twelve to sixteen interviewed Cecily von Ziegesar. During the interview, fifteen-year-old Hanna asked von Ziegesar: "If you have teenagers, or have had teenagers, would you let them read this book? If so, would you let them read it as a 'what not to do' lesson or as a 'see what Mommy does in her spare time'?"

Von Ziegesar replied: "I have a two-year-old daughter and a baby boy on the way—eventually they will be teenagers. I'll let them read the books when and if they're interested and just wait and see what they have to say. I don't think I'm going to be the type of parent who forbids her kids to read certain books or see certain movies or wear certain clothes or whatever. I'd rather let my kids see what's out there and make their own opinions and choices."[7]

Much like the revisions to this book, Ms. von Ziegesar wanted to revisit the first book in the series to update it and keep it current. "It occurred to me that there are so many opportunities in that novel to have people die, because everyone is mad at everyone else," she says. "It was a matter of taking it one step further. It's not meant to be taken seriously—it's like the b**** are back and now they have knives! Instead of brushing their kids' bad behavior under the rug, the adults are now brushing murders under the rug."[8] The outcome, *Psycho Killer*, is a tongue-in-cheek reimagining of the original that glamorizes beautiful, rich girls who supposedly have everything— who go crazy, and sardonically, killing becomes a competition between them.[9]

I'd like to talk with Ms. von Ziegesar when her daughter is fifteen and see if her opinion has changed. I think Samuel Taylor Coleridge, the great English poet of the Romantic period, would suggest the same thought to Ms. von Ziegesar that he once offered to a man who told him he did not believe in giving religious instruction to children. The man believed children's minds should not be prejudiced in any direction, so that when the children were able to think for themselves, they would be able to choose their religious opinions for themselves. Coleridge didn't respond, but after a while he asked his visitor if he would like to see his garden. The man said he would, and Coleridge took him out into the garden, where only weeds were growing. The man said, "Why, this is not a garden! There are nothing but weeds here!"

"Well, you see," answered Coleridge. "I did not wish to infringe upon the liberty of the garden in any way. I was just giving the garden a chance to express itself and to choose its own production."[10]

Unfortunately, Ms. von Ziegesar is not the only mom who's unwilling to protect her treasures from the trash. Many mothers are saying they're not concerned about the content in the *Gossip Girl* series because these books have helped their daughters develop a love for reading. (Sounds like the scheme of the enemy—enticement with legitimacy to mask the hidden immorality.)

Not only have the books gained greater popularity, but the television series ran for six seasons. But there *is* one set of parents that did something in their community.

Parents Who Did Something

IN THE SMALL TOWN OF Picayune, Mississippi, Mr. and Mrs. Tony Smith decided to "take action" when their thirteen-year-old daughter brought a copy of *Nobody Does It Better*, the seventh book in the *Gossip Girl* series, home from her junior high school's library. The cover of the book grabbed the attention of Mrs. Smith. Horrified by the use of the "f" word and the "s" word and the sexual content of the book, she asked her husband, then chairman of the Picayune School Board, what could be done.

After hearing Mrs. Smith's concerns, the decision was made to remove the books from all the school libraries in the district. Much to the Smiths' dismay, they discovered the *Gossip Girls* books were on the advanced Reader Selection list used by schools around the country.

After talking to school librarians, they found that salesmen pitch the top-selling books knowing most librarians are concerned with staying current. Tony Smith, now a state senator, has drafted legislation concerning the process for how books are selected for school libraries.[11]

It takes only one set of parents willing to do something to get the ball rolling back in the right direction.

Harry Potter, Move Over

IN 2005, A NEW "KID" in town captured the hearts of teenage girls and the imaginations of teenage boys. His name: Edward Cullen. Not a young man himself, Edward is a 104-year-old vampire, the love interest of Isabella "Bella" Swan, the teenage protagonist of *Twilight*. Critics often described it as a "dark romance that seeps into the soul." Three more books have followed, each continuing the theme of a teenage love obsession in which a young woman is willing to throw away her family, friends, and herself to be with "the man of her dreams," regardless of the cost.

In 2008, a new chart-buster hit the market for young adults, *The Hunger Games*. If young adults were the only ones reading it, I wouldn't feel compelled to say much, but tweens and teens are reading it as well. In the last ten years or so, literature for children has become darker and tougher, with more graphic violence, as evidenced by this series.

I strongly believe that as parents we must consider the subtle, and not-so-subtle, messages our kids are receiving through the books they read. We have to make judgment calls about the intent behind the words. Don't make the mistake of focusing solely on the storyline in the books your children read. You need to look at the messages being communicated through the actions and behaviors of the characters in these stories. We must read between the lines.

Not only do we need to look at the messages between the words, but even more important, the worldview of the author. As a writer, I know all too well the influence my worldview takes in my writing. Woven into every sentence, even without conscious thought, is the desire to present truth. The intention of *The Chronicles of Narnia* by C. S. Lewis is clear, because we know the heart of the author. Do we know the intent behind the authors of the aforementioned series? To entertain? To teach a moral lesson? To persuade? To frighten? To portray admirable human qualities? To help teenagers make wise choices?

Rest assured, the worldview of the author is critically important. Think of C. S. Lewis, Mark Twain, Charles Dickens, J.R.R. Tolkien—these authors delivered works that offer the right stuff. Entertainment. Imaginative writing. Resolution of the human condition. Ultimately, redemption.

The trouble with the *Gossip Girl* series is obvious—blatant disrespect for society, God, and all things decent. The *Twilight* series places Bella in a terribly vulnerable position, not unlike what many teenage girls experience when it comes to young love. Is her plight resolved in a healthy way that gives the reader a viable answer for her life?

> **Books** for children should contain nothing to cause fright, suggest fear, glorify mischief, excuse malice, or condone cruelty.
>
> —Johnny Gruelle, creator of Raggedy Ann

Think of the influence the written word has had in your life when considering the books you place in your children's hands.

And what about the music that's found alongside the books and magazines in the stores?

Disrespectful Messages in Music

MY FATHER'S TASTE IN MUSIC ran from classic to country. Before we kids could make our way to the living room on Christmas morning, Daddy already had the music going. His favorite Christmas tunes came from Perry Como, Johnny Cash, and Alvin and the Chipmunks.

When I was in high school, he called rock-and-roll "ya, ya, ya racket" because he couldn't understand the words. But he was even more upset by the beat. "The rhythm makes you feel things you should only feel in the bedroom with your wife," he would say with utter disgust. I found myself echoing his disgust the day I called the music of this generation "ya, ya, ya garbage."

Once upon a time, music inspired love to blossom. Nat King Cole's "Unforgettable" touched the heart with the tender sentiment that love is a unique experience. "When I Fall in Love" spoke of the one true love that lasts forever. Lyrics encouraged love with one special someone.

> Kids are looking for an ***identity***, and there is a huge mass-media machine eager to give them one— one that has nothing to do with reality. If you are a Christian, of course you want your child to have a Christ-centered identity, but you need to know that the culture-centered identity is the exact opposite.
>
> —Bob Just, "'Killer Culture': A Call to the Churches"

But along with the sweet songs, the rock-and-roll invasion took place. The biggest names found their way to *The Ed Sullivan Show*. Still, behind the scenes it didn't matter who the band was— they were expected to tow the line of decency. In 1967, The Rolling Stones were asked by *The Ed Sullivan Show* to change the lyrics of their hit song from "Let's Spend the Night Together" to "Let's Spend Some Time Together." Out of respect for Ed Sullivan, they acquiesced and were invited to return. Later that same year, a controversy arose with a line from "Light My Fire" by The Doors. In contrast to The Rolling Stones, they refused to remove "Girl, we couldn't get much higher," which Sullivan felt implied drug use. The Doors never again appeared on his show.

How standards for what's acceptable in music have changed! Now, no topic is taboo, from free sex to masturbation to sadomasochism, and whatever would be in between. Many of today's top pop stars started out as "innocent girls" who "sexed up" their acts to increase record sales. Today's lyrics are filled with a word that begins with the letter *f*. It's even in the titles of songs by R&B crooner Eamon and the hip-hop artists OutKast. Twenty years ago these folks would not have been allowed on any stage anywhere in our country. Today they perform before sold-out audiences.

In 1985 a group of United States senators' wives, believing that the decay of the nuclear family was attributable, at least in part, to the disrespectful lyrics in rock music, formed the Parents Music Resource Center to combat the problem. They demanded a method for warning parents of the dangerous material contained in the lyrics of songs of the music groups their kids were listening to. Even though the Recording Industry Association of America (RIAA) objected, along with recording artists Frank Zappa and Rage Against the Machine, PMRC succeeded in their goal of requiring the labeling of records that contained "explicit lyrics or content."[12]

But the situation has continued to degenerate. Some groups originally opposed to the record labeling are beginning to admit something does need to be done. We can only hope the RIAA will decide to self-police, but in the meantime we can't hold our breath

> Whatever ***purifies*** the heart also fortifies it.
>
> —Hugh Blair

waiting, because we'll all pass out, and then where will our children be?

In a recent interview about the disrespectful world, a radio commentator asked me, "So, Jill, don't you think the line has been crossed this time? I mean, really, the line has finally been crossed. Don't you think?"

"No, I don't think a line has been crossed."

"Come on, Jill, even I think this one is just too much," he said in amazement.

"The line hasn't been crossed, because no one has drawn the line. That's the problem!" I retorted, making my point.

Who is drawing the line? Society's not drawing the line. Neither is the music industry. So parents must draw the line.

Help for Knowing When and How to Draw the Line

BLAST FROM THE PAST IS a delightful movie set in the sixties that has become a classic. Adam, a handsome young man with a heart of gold, was born in the bomb shelter of his genius inventor dad, who convinced his pregnant wife that they should go underground when he thought our country had been hit by a nuclear bomb. Stocked with enough supplies to last thirty-five years, the couple raised their son, Adam, with values that were untarnished by influences of the changing world above. Adam's mother taught him manners, how to dance, and the importance of being polite. His dad taught him about baseball, science, and the pitfalls of the seedier side of life.

When Adam leaves his underground home and goes to the surface, the young man's character is tested. But rather than being changed by the world, Adam changes those he meets. His sense of duty and honor to his family supersedes the temptations to indulge in the things of the world.

Granted, you and I can't raise our children in bomb shelters, nor would we want to, but we can put a shield of protection around them, keeping the bad influences from damaging their character. We can help our children become adults who change the world. How? By spending more time teaching them the "better way."

Here are a few suggestions for how you can do just that:

Model Godly Reading and Listening Choices

DON'T COUNT ON THAT OLD adage—"Do as I say, not as I do." It didn't work with us, did it? Children will do what you do. What one generation condones, the next will accept, so don't read or listen to anything you don't want them to read or listen to. Do your kids see you regularly reading the bestseller of all time? More than three billion copies have been sold—the *Holy Bible*. And the music that's in your home . . . is it sexy or serene?

Don't Allow Free Choice in Entertainment

MAKE IT CLEAR THAT THE magazines, books, and music enjoyed by members of your family will promote good values. Let your children know that if it's not fit for you to hear, then it's not fit for them to hear. If it's not fit for you to see, then it's not fit for them to see.

Open Your Children's Eyes to the Best of Culture

EXPOSE THEM TO IMAGES AND values that show the good in our society—timeless treasures that embody the good of humankind, not the depravity. For example:

1. When you first begin reading to your children, *read Bible stories together*. Young boys enjoy hearing about David and Goliath, and the story shows that when we are armed with God's truth for protection, we can stand against giants. The story of Esther teaches girls that beauty is only skin deep, that much more important than beauty is the willingness to be courageous when given an opportunity to help others. God protected Shadrach, Meshach, and Abednego, who

refused to bow in worship to false gods. They were tossed into a fiery furnace, but God walked with them, and they were not burned. What life lessons to teach your children!

2. *Visit used bookstores, and buy old children's books to read to your kids.* Look for old school readers, such as *My Little Red Story Book*, *At Work and Play*, and the Mac and Muff series. Pre-sixties readers often mingled Bible stories with stories of Dick and Jane.

3. *Introduce your children to classical music,* even if it's not your taste in music. If we don't first expose them to a better alternative, our kids will choose what others expose them to.

4. *Take your children to museums.* Fill their minds with images of fine art. When we lived in New York City, my boys were in preschool, and I often took them to museums. What a blessing this turned out to be for my sons! They developed an appreciation for art at an early age. They also developed respect for the work of others, respect for public places, and respect for rules.

5. *Use Scripture to teach middle-school children the importance of what we see and what we hear and how it affects our souls.* Your thirteen-year-old needs to know that your opinion matters, but God's opinion counts the most. Read passages such as:

> For everything in the world—the cravings of sinful man, the lust of his eyes and the boasting of what he has and does—comes not from the Father but from the world. The world and its desires pass away, but the man who does the will of God lives forever. [13]

Many are the plans in a man's heart, but it is the Lord's purpose that prevails.[14]

"For I know the plans I have for you," declares the Lord, "plans to prosper you and not to harm you, plans to give you hope and a future."[15]

I urge you, brothers, to watch out for those who cause divisions and put obstacles in your way that are contrary to the teaching you have learned. Keep away from them. For such people are not serving our Lord Christ, but their own appetites. By smooth talk and flattery they deceive the minds of naive people. Everyone has heard about your obedience, so I am full of joy over you; but I want you to be wise about what is good, and innocent about what is evil.[16]

Finally, brothers, whatever is true, whatever is noble, whatever is right, whatever is pure, whatever is lovely, whatever is admirable—if anything is excellent or praiseworthy—think about such things.[17]

6. *Encourage high school kids to choose the better way.* High school teens are most vulnerable to the messages of the trash, if the foundation has not been laid to understand its influence. Fortify your teens with the truth that:

+ Every decision you make means choosing one thing over another.

+ Teens respect other teens who stand their ground against the trash.

Evie was a high school student who made a decision to not become infected by the culture. She chose to live her life according to God's principles, regardless of ridicule. But rather than being alienated, she was elevated to homecoming queen by the votes of her classmates because of the great respect she commanded. Evie found that sharing God's love with fellow students without succumbing to the temptations of following the crowd was the better way.

✦ The friends you choose to surround yourself with today affect who you will become tomorrow.

7. *Do your part to encourage your children's school to offer only the "good stuff."* It's not enough to work hard in your home to expose your children to the good stuff; your kids need to see that your commitment goes beyond the walls of your home. They need to see that you're willing to go out on a limb in our society for their sakes. Follow my mother's lead.

She had *Seventeen* magazine removed from our high school library in 1972 because of an article about teenage sex. She calmly walked into the principal's office with a copy of the magazine and asked if he would want his daughter to read the article or, even worse, if he would want his daughter's date to read it. The principal agreed and had the magazine removed.

Do you want to raise respectful children in a disrespectful world? Then saturate their minds with the right stuff, the good stuff the world has to offer. By doing this, you will not only be shielding your treasures from the trash, you'll be training them to discern for themselves what is worthy of their time and interest, especially if they see you take a stand for the right against the wrong. When your kids respect you, they are on their way to becoming respectful adults.

In the next chapter, we'll take a look at how you can protect your treasures from the trash that permeates movies, TV, video games, and the Internet.

9

Shield Your Treasures from the Trash:

Movies, TV, Video Games, and the Internet

HERE WE ARE, seven years past the breakdown of the levees around New Orleans. The largest flood disaster in U.S. history, its cleanup costs topped $110 billion. Some 275,000 homes were destroyed and more than 1,100 lives were taken, with another 705 people still missing.[1] The rebuilding process continues today, with some neighborhoods still as they were a year after the storm.

One of the engineers involved in the cleanup said, "It was fully recognized by officials we had a Category Three level of protection. We were caught by a storm whose intensity exceeded the protection we had in place."[2] Fifty years ago, no one could conceive of the enormity of the storms to come.

Throughout the Midwest along the upper Mississippi River, many communities are protected from destructive floods by levee systems of varying sizes. Another large and potentially vulnerable system is a vital freshwater conduit from Northern California through the state's Central Valley and on to Southern California, housed in the California Delta.[3]

Cities and communities across our country are watching old levees, no longer strong enough to keep dangerous waters at bay, begin to crumble. Prevention is too often minimized until the threats are more tangible, until people can imagine their results. At that point, it is often too late to avoid a large loss.[4]

Much in our culture has changed fifty years after self-esteem made landfall in the late sixties. Concerns are present today that were nonexistent a few short years ago. Just as the levees are no longer dependable, neither can we depend on the "powers that be" to build protections around our children's innocence. The movie industry and television networks have lost sight of their responsibility to offer quality productions that encourage respect and civility. Sensationalism has replaced common decency.

With the explosion of mobile devices (as I write, the world awaits the arrival of the next iPhone), the Internet is now in the hands of our children, not just sitting on a desk in your living room. This generation is all too quickly becoming "The Wireless Generation," disconnected from all things good.

But there is hope. In this chapter, you'll find ways to protect and fortify your children from the media-driven age that threatens their safe passage into adolescence and later, into adulthood. If you're willing to rebuild a wall of protection around your children, you will be able to teach your children how to discern for themselves what is good and noble and true.

✳   ✳   ✳

WANT TO KNOW A SURE sign your child is watching too much television? Watching too many movies? Playing too many video games? Spending too much time on the computer?

See if one of the following scenarios rings a bit too familiar:

"No! Don't . . . it's not over," cries ten-year-old Chuck.

"Darling, it's time to read," Mom says calmly.

"But I have to see the end of the show." Or,

"But I don't wanna read a dumb old book. Books just stare at you . . . they're boring."

"I'm in a chat room . . . I gotta wait for the end of this . . . can't you see this is important?"

If you've had these kinds of arguments in your home, it's time to reassess the amount of time your child is spending in front of these screens. And just as important, what's on those screens.

Many of today's children are oversaturated with the images and messages they see in movies, on television, and on the Web. These screens can program our youth to accept deviant behavior as normal, view violence as an ordinary part of living, and believe that fantasy is reality. In this chapter we are going to examine the disrespectful messages found in movies, TV, video games, and the Internet, and then we'll discuss what you can do to protect your kids from these messages.

Disrespectful Messages in Movies

FANTASY BECOMES REALITY WHEN CHARACTERS become larger than life on the big screen, and unfortunately, our kids often base their decisions about what's right and wrong on the movies.

Just as drug dealers know an addict needs more of a drug than the hit before to satisfy his habit, movie producers continue to deepen our addiction for drama and violence. With each new movie, the violence is more intense and the message of good versus evil becomes more blurred. *Harry Potter* did it; *Star Wars* did it. The last release of each was described by critics as "darker." Let's hope *Indiana Jones* does not follow their lead if George Lucas brings Indy back to the big screen for a final run. Lucas, the genius behind *Star Wars*, received "a lot of flak" from parents concerned about the PG-13 rating of *Revenge of the Sith* when it was released a few years ago. "A lot of people were saying, how can you do this? My children love these movies. Why can you not let them go see it?" Lucas said. "But I have to tell a story. I'm not making these, oddly enough, to be giant, successful blockbusters. I'm making them because I'm telling a story, and I have to tell the story I intended."[5]

But why did Mr. Lucas not consider his audience when making the film? It's distressing to think he was making those films to satisfy his need to tell a story rather than telling a story that children would enjoy watching. Those with significant influence over children too often dismiss the responsibility that comes with their influence. It doesn't matter whether they like having the responsibility or not. They have it, and that's what matters.

The ratings in films are supposedly meant to help parents discern their appropriateness, but the ratings are flawed. A study by the Kids Risk Project at the Harvard School of Public Health found "that ratings creep has occurred over the last decade and that today's movies contain significantly more violence, sex, and profanity on average than movies of the same rating a decade ago."[6]

Could it be that in 1992, the third episode of *Star Wars* would have received an R rating?

Dr. Thompson of the Harvard group would argue, yes. Others agree. The Kids-in-Mind group contends that the Motion Picture Association of America ratings are not accurate. Financed by the film industry, the MPAA doesn't function as an independent agent but is controlled by the moviemakers, therefore making the ratings negotiable.

An additional caution to parents concerning the MPAA ratings system is that ratings are age specific, not content specific, which allows for a wide variance in opinion of what is appropriate or not. Factors beyond sex and violence are often overlooked.

The vampire obsession discussed in the previous chapter continued to the big screen. The last of the series was released in November of 2012, but *The Hunger Games* took over as the teen hit of the summer. Unlike the *Twilight* series, the *Hunger Games* trilogy, by Suzanne Collins, straddles the line between dark and hopeful, but the violence of kids killing kids is impossible to get past.

For me, the determining factor in appropriate or inappropriate movies for my sons was what I called the "R" factor, not to be confused with the "R" rating. The movie had to pass this test question:

Is the movie I'm allowing my children to see Redeeming, Refreshing, and Respectful? If I could give the movie a 3R rating, it was a go. If not, it was a no-go. (By the way, the three R rule also stood for Rigby, Rigby, and Rigby . . . Boyce, Chad, and Jill!)

What's a Parent to Do?

DURING THE SPECIAL STUDY WE conducted among children of varying ages, we asked a series of questions about their movie-viewing habits:

+ Have you watched an R-rated film; if so, how often?

+ Who allowed you to see it? Your parents, siblings, or friends?

✦ Have you watched a PG-13 movie; if so, how often?

✦ Who allowed you to see it? Your parents, siblings, or friends?

We were astonished to find kids as young as six who had watched R-rated movies. Seventy-five percent of twelve-year-olds watched R-rated movies at least once a month. Ninety percent of seven-year-olds watched PG-13 movies regularly. (Remember, the PG-13 movie of today would have received an R rating just twelve years ago.) More than 65 percent said their parents were the ones who allowed them to see these movies.

As parents, our first priority should be protecting our kids from the disrespectful messages in films. We all have different opinions on what is appropriate and what is not. If you trust others to make that decision for you, it could prove harmful to your child. I recommend that you see the movie you have any doubts about before you allow your children to see it. Do your homework. We can all be fooled.

I learned this lesson the hard way the night I took my sons to a PG-13 movie. (They were fourteen, and I had received reliable reports that the movie was a good choice, but I didn't check it out myself before I took them.) Without warning, a scene I deemed inappropriate appeared on the big screen. I was seated between them and reached on either side to cover their eyes. But my hands became entangled with theirs as they attempted to cover my eyes. "Mom, you shouldn't see this!" they said in unison.

"If I shouldn't see it, then you shouldn't see it . . . right?" I responded with a sixth-grade-teacher look. "Get the point?"

They nodded in agreement.

Our second priority should be to do something about the movie industry. If we parents voiced our opinions so the film industry could hear us, we could make a difference. Why do we allow the industry to dictate to us, rather than telling it what we would like to see? We, the consumers, hold the power. The problem is that we're not exercising our power. If we want to raise respectful children, we can make our job easier by working to change the disrespectful world . . . starting with the movie industry.

Let me offer a suggestion for how you can help transform the disrespectful world. Start in your own home. Put up your shield and don't let it down. Raise awareness that we're not helpless victims by working with those organizations involved in trying to change our culture. Here are a few of the best:

✦ *Citizens for Community Values* (CCV): www.ccv.org
> Phil and Vickie Burress are dedicated to the return of moral values in our country. What began as an effort to remove the pornography industry from their city has grown into a national organization combating the entertainment industry and affecting legislation in Washington, D.C.

✦ *Family Research Council* (FRC): www.frc.org
> Located in the heart of our capital, FRC has long been a driving force for the good of the family in our country. This organization uses its influence to promote sound moral principles in all areas of society. Of particular note is the work they do on Capitol Hill as the voice for the family in legislative issues.

✦ *State Family Policy Councils*: www.citizenlink.com
> As of this writing, thirty-six states have an established family policy council, with more being added each year. Visit the website to find a council or start one in your state! You can also sign up for a yearly subscription to *Citizen* magazine, a great resource for combating the entertainment industry. I am hon-

ored to serve on the board of the Louisiana Family
Forum, the advocacy group in our state that speaks
as the voice for families desiring to return our society to the moral standards of the past.

✦ *The Agape Press*: www.onenewsnow.com
Excellent source for updates on the latest news af-
fecting your family. Visit their website to sign up for
a daily bulletin.

✦ *American Family Association* (AFA): www.afa.net
Today, AFA is one of the largest and most effective
pro-family organizations in the country, with over
two million online supporters and approximately
180,000 paid subscribers to the *AFA Journal*, the
ministry's monthly magazine. In addition, AFA
owns and operates nearly two hundred radio sta-
tions across the country under the American Family
Radio (AFR) banner. AFA also maintains two ac-
tivist websites, OneMillionMoms.com and OneMi-
llionDads.com. I encourage you to visit these sites
and sign up for AFA Action Alerts to keep abreast
of emerging cultural issues that affect the moral-
ity of the country as well as the family and media.
When called to action, act! You'll be surprised how
many folks in your local community are just waiting
for someone to take the first step. You won't stand
alone when you take a stand.

You'll need all the help you can get, because the movies aren't
the only source of wrong messages.

Disrespectful Messages on TV and in Video Games

DISRESPECTFULNESS *IS* RAMPANT, NOT ONLY on the big screen, but during prime time on the little screens (which aren't always so little anymore). Let me show you what I mean.

In 2006, I used *Desperate Housewives* as an example of disrespectfulness on television. Seems it paved the way for shows gone wild. Today, *Carrie's Diaries* chronicles the actions of a sixteen-year-old girl looking for answers to life while interning at a New York City law firm. Surrounded by characters as lost as she is, the show is a prequel to *Sex in the City*.

In August 2012, the Parents Television Council (PTC) released a study looking at nudity on prime-time broadcast television. The study found there were seventy-six incidents of full nudity on thirty-seven shows compared to fifteen incidents in fourteen shows the previous ratings season, representing a 407 percent increase. And to make matters worse, 70 percent of the scenes were aired prior to 9:00 p.m. (And to think in the first edition I was lamenting Janet Jackson's "wardrobe malfunction" during the 2004 Super Bowl halftime show!)[7] The most disturbing finding was in regard to full-frontal nudity. No incidents occurred the year this book came out (2006). One incident occurred during 2011. In 2012, sixty-four full-frontal incidences occurred, a 6,300 percent increase. Melissa Henson, Director of Communications for PTC, told FOX411's Pop Tarts, "For years executives at the broadcast networks have been telegraphing their intent to follow in the footsteps of premium cable networks like HBO. They have been aggressively increasing the amount and explicitness of sexual content, nudity, foul language and violence in their primetime offerings. In just two years there has been a 400 percent increase."[8]

TV sitcoms have gone to a deeper level of disrespectfulness. CBS, the Monday-night king of comedy, airs four of the top seven sitcoms. Here is a sampling of one night in January 2012:

✦ *How I Met Your Mother* featured a strip club with lap dance.

✦ *2 Broke Girls* focused on a supposed brothel in the main characters' building with discussions about anal sex.

✦ *Two and a Half Men* included jokes on masturbation, oral sex, sex with moms, and trading cigarettes for sex.

✦ *Mike & Molly* portrayed two scenes with marijuana, one with a teenage boy and another with an older woman.[9]

During just two hours of broadcasting, fifty-three sex jokes and nine jokes about flatulence/bowel movements were blurted, in addition to the above. When Michael Patrick King, creator of *2 Broke Girls*, was questioned about the raunchiness of his show, he responded, "It's 8:30 on Monday on CBS in 2012. It's a very different world than 8:30 on Monday on CBS in 1994. . . . I consider our jokes really classy dirty. I think they're high lowbrow. I think they're fun and sophisticated and naughty, and I think everybody likes a good naughty joke."[10]

I hope you would agree with me there's no such thing as "classy dirty." There's dirty or classy, not both.

Speaking of dirty . . . in the world of teen television, four MTV shows ranked as the most-watched by twelve- to seventeen-year-olds during the 2011 season: *Jersey Shore, Real World, Teen Mom 2,* and *16 and Pregnant*. Take a look at the content:

✦ Females were the recipients of an "f-word" or "s-word" 662 times, or once every four minutes and ten seconds.

✦ Females talked about sex acts more than men, talked about sex more graphically than men, mentioned sexual body parts more than men, and talked about intercourse and preliminaries to intercourse more than men.

✦ Although 88 percent of the sexual dialogue between females and males across all shows focused on intercourse and preliminary activities leading to intercourse (e.g., foreplay), the topics of virginity (0.2 percent), contraceptives (1.4 percent), and STDs (2 percent) were mentioned only 4 percent of the time out of all the shows combined.

✦ There was no difference in the most popular derogatory terms females used to talk about other females compared to the most popular derogatory terms males used to talk about females. These terms represent the most popular derogatory terms used to refer to females across all shows:

  ✦ B****

  ✦ Stupid

  ✦ Dirty[11]

Yep, there's that word "dirty" again. No such thing as "classy dirty." Just dirty.

Speaking of MTV . . . Nickelodeon was launched as the children's network in 1979 to offer quality children's programming. But that was more than thirty years ago. Today, Nickelodeon is a feeder station for MTV (one of the most disrespectful channels on television) as part of the Viacom empire. That's why most of the programs on Nickelodeon are unsuitable for young viewers; they're being led down the path to become MTVholics when they turn twelve. Even the couple of good shows for young children are tarnished because of the advertising that opens and closes each episode. It's an old salesman's trick . . . just get them in the front door so they'll stay awhile and buy more. Don't believe me? You don't have to take my word for it.

Leonard J. Beer, editor in chief of *Hits* magazine, a music industry trade publication, had this to say in an interview with *Frontline*:

> I'm very pro-MTV. I think MTV has probably created the best brand in television that anybody's ever created. The MTV networks make zillions of dollars. They own the kids almost from the time they come out of the fetus, you know. My kids grew up watching Nickelodeon and got moved into the MTV networks, and you know, it's the cultural beat of their generation. And it has been since the day it went on the air.[12]

Are your kids watching? If so, pay attention to these cold, hard facts:

+ Eight- to eighteen-year-olds devote an average of seven hours and thirty-eight minutes to using entertainment media across a typical day (more than fifty-three hours a week). And because they spend so much of that time "media multitasking" (using more than one medium at a time), they actually manage to pack a total of ten hours and forty-five minutes worth of media content into those seven and a half hours.[13]

+ On average, music videos contain ninety-three sexual situations per hour, including eleven "hard-core" scenes depicting behaviors such as intercourse and oral sex.[14]

+ Before the age of eighteen, the average child will witness over 200,000 acts of violence on television, including 16,000 murders.[15]

+ Riot Games' "League of Legends" is the most played PC game in North America and Europe, with gamers logging more than 1.3 billion hours of play from July 2011 to July 2012.[16]

+ Teens who watch more sexual content on television are more likely to initiate intercourse and progress to more advanced noncoital sexual activities during the subsequent year.[17]

+ Average time American kids spend watching television each day: four hours.

+ Nearly one in three infants through one-year-olds (30 percent) have a TV in their bedroom. In 2005, among children ages six to twenty-three months, 19 percent had a TV in their bedroom. Looking just at six- to twenty-three-month-olds in the current study, 29 percent have a TV in their bedroom.[18]

+ Forty-seven percent of babies and toddlers ages zero through one watch TV or DVDs, and those who watch spend an average of nearly two hours a day doing so, compared to an average of 23 percent being read to.[19]

I won't hit you with any more statistics. You know how bad it is. So how does all this affect our children? A noted pediatric surgeon has a strong opinion. Dr. Lorraine Day has advocated the elimination of TV viewing by children under the age of two for several years. Through her years of research, she has found that:

Children watch an average of 43 hours of TV per week; that's longer than the average adult work week. While watching, they rapidly become almost hypnotized. It has been shown scientifically that within minutes of beginning to watch TV, the brain changes from the alert brain waves (beta waves) to the hypnotic waves (alpha waves) where the judgment center of the brain is bypassed. So the violence and decadence that the child sees bypasses the judgment center in the brain and is implanted in the child's brain without any ability on the child's part to decide whether what they are seeing is right or wrong. The violence and decadence are accepted by the brain without any moral judgment being applied to it. It then becomes part of the child's permanent subconscious.[20]

I hope Dr. Day has convinced you to turn off the television. We do have control over that remote, if we will only exercise it. I regret that I allowed my own sons to watch too much television when they were younger. If I had it to do over again, I would turn it off much sooner.

For **reliable** information on children's television, visit: http://www.parentstv.org.

What's a Parent to Do?

I'M ALWAYS LOOKING FOR THE disconnect—the place where our understanding of a problem doesn't match our actions. The truth is, we don't practice what we preach. According to a recent survey by the Pew Research Center, 75 percent of adults polled would like to see tighter enforcement of government standards for broadcast content during hours children are watching.[21] *Time* magazine recently reported that 68 percent of respondents to a poll said they believe the entertainment industry has lost touch with viewers' moral standards. Fifty percent said there's too much sexual content on TV.[22]

Do you see the discrepancies between what many parents are saying and what they are actually doing? The most vulgar show on network television is number one, yet 50 percent of viewers *say* there's too much sex on TV. Seventy-five percent of adults *say* they want tighter controls to protect children's viewing, but the shows they allow their kids to watch are *Jersey Shore, 2 Broke Girls,* and *Two and a Half Men.*

We say one thing and do another. We still want someone else to make the hard decisions for us. I'm just as guilty as anyone else. But it's time we stand up and say, "Enough!"

Here are some ways you can say, "Enough!":

1. *Monitor your children's entertainment choices.* I'm not advocating no television at all, although I do have friends who have chosen that option and enjoy the tranquility a great deal. I am advocating the careful, systematic monitoring of every minute the box is turned on.

   For children younger than two, the questionable benefits of television don't outweigh the negative effects. Why set your kids up for attention deficit problems? It's much more important that toddlers work on cognitive and motor skills than sit in front of a box. The American Academy of Pediatrics recommends no television for children under the age of two.

2. *Practice what you preach, and turn off your television.* It's not okay for you and your spouse to watch *Jersey Shore* with children in your home. We can't blame the media if we're watching what they give us to watch. See Chapter 10 for things you can do with your kids to keep them engaged and their TV watching to a bare minimum.

3. *Complain to the Federal Communications Commission (FCC) regarding the subject matter seen in television.* The regulation of obscenity, indecency, and profanity on television falls under their domain. According to their website, "It is a violation of federal law to air obscene programming at any time. It is also a violation of federal law to broadcast indecent or profane

programming during certain hours."[23] The FCC has received more than 1.6 million unexamined indecency complaints, but that has not been enough to show the public's disgust with programming infractions. We need to do more, much more.

You can contact the FCC one of four ways:

1. U.S. Postal Service:
   FCC
   Enforcement Bureau, Investigations and
       Hearings Division
   445 12th Street, S.W.
   Washington, D.C. 20554

2. E-mail: fccinfo@fcc.gov

3. Toll free: 1-888-CALL-FCC (1-888-225-5322)

4. Fax: 1-888-418-0232

The FCC promises all complaints will be read and addressed within nine months of receipt. There is much evidence to support that the FCC does not address complaints as promised, but we must continue to find ways to make our voices heard. All I have to do is look in the eyes of my grandchildren to keep myself involved. I want to protect their innocence to the greatest degree possible.

Last in our look at the disrespectful messages of the entertainment industry is the invasion of the Internet. It's the most damaging of all, with repercussions that can last a lifetime.

Disrespectful Messages on the Internet

DISRESPECTFUL MESSAGES ABOUND ON THE World Wide Web. First, I'm going to focus our attention on pornography because of the astounding number of pornographic websites and chat rooms. Sadly, many adults have been preconditioned to hard-core pornography through the soft porn on television and in the movies. The constant bombardment of sexual images has programmed many adults to accept as normal behavior what was once considered taboo.

Pornography addiction is epidemic in our society. I'll let the numbers speak for themselves:

+ Porn revenue is larger than combined revenues of all professional football, baseball, and basketball franchises ($54 billion).[24] Here is a breakdown (all figures are annual):

Adult videos	$20 billion
Magazines	$7.5 billion
Cable and Pay-Per-View	$2.5 billion
Internet	$2.5 billion
Child pornography	$3 billion

In addition, $19.5 billion is spent on everything from sex clubs to novelties.

+ There are 4.2 billion pornographic websites.

+ Number of daily pornographic e-mails: 2.5 billion (8 percent of total e-mails)

+ Websites offering illegal child pornography: 100,000

+ Percentage of solicitations in chat rooms made to underage visitors: 89 percent

+ Worldwide visitors to pornographic websites: 72 million annually

+ Average age of first Internet exposure to pornography: eleven

+ Largest consumers of Internet pornography: twelve- to seventeen-year olds

+ Fifteen- to seventeen-year-olds having multiple hard-core exposures: 80 percent

+ Eight- to sixteen-year-olds having viewed porn online: 90 percent

+ Seven- to seventeen-year-olds who would freely give out their e-mail address: 14 percent[25]

In his book *The Disappearance of Childhood*, Neil Postman, one of our country's foremost cultural critics, points out "that over-exposure to adult information at a young age robs a child of his innocence."[26] Don't you agree? Remember the girl in Chapter 2 whose father took her to see an exploitative R-rated movie? After viewing the movie, she said, "I thought if I asked God to forgive me, I wouldn't see the pictures anymore . . . and I'd forget the words, but they won't go away." This is what happens to children when they're exposed to too much too early—their innocence disappears.

Here we are again. Discouraged by devastating information, and yet, as parents, we have no choice but to do our best to prevent our children from being exposed to inappropriate material. The National Research Council offers these tips for how parents can protect and educate children about Internet pornography:

+ Allow your kids access only to Web pages that you have already checked and found safe.

+ Block inappropriate material with filtering software.

+ Monitor your children's Web activity and impose a penalty if they are caught visiting unapproved sites.

+ Warn your kids about explicit material and suggest they choose something better.

+ Educate your children about reasons not to view explicit material, and build their sense of responsibility.[27]

If you or your spouse are struggling with pornography, it will affect your decisions concerning what you allow your children to see. Confess to a trusted friend that you're struggling. This may sound easy, but it's not if you're the one who has to admit you're having trouble. Pornography gains a stronghold on individuals because it's the "secret addiction" until it begins to manifest itself in extramarital affairs and much worse. Ask for help to overcome it, and with God's help and your conviction to not allow pornography to ruin your marriage and your family, you will be able to do it.

Meanwhile, even as the **Internet** has become the principal means of distributing child pornography, it has become all but undeniable that it is a significant factor in the sexual exploitation of children. For instance, the Los Angeles Police Department has conducted a ten-year study that found pornography to be a factor in 62 percent of the cases of child molestation.

An FBI study of serial killers shows that 81 percent reported hard-core pornography to be their "highest sexual interest."[28]

—Kelly Patricia O'Meara

Unfortunately, there are two more areas of concern that were almost nonexistent in 2006 that we need to discuss: social media and smartphones.

Social Media and Teens

SOCIAL MEDIA USE HAS BECOME so pervasive in the lives of American teens that having a presence on a social network site is almost synonymous with being online. Fully 95 percent of all young people ages twelve to seventeen are now online, and 80 percent of them are users of social media sites.[29]

Among the teens using social media, 88 percent report having seen someone be mean or cruel to another person on a social network site. Social media use does affect how some teens interact with one another. Nearly one-third (31 percent) of teenage social media users say they've flirted with someone online that they wouldn't have flirted with in person, and 25 percent say they've said something bad about someone online that they wouldn't have said in person.[30]

Let me give you a few statistics of online practices that have the potential to compromise your teen's safety:

✦ 44 percent of online teens admit to lying about their age so they could access a website or sign up for an online account.

✦ 30 percent of online teens report sharing one of their passwords with a friend, boyfriend, or girlfriend.

✦ 47 percent of online girls ages fourteen to seventeen say they have shared their passwords, compared with 27 percent of boys the same age.[31]

Smartphones, Tablets, and Texting

THE MOST DRAMATIC CHANGE IN media use since the publication of the first book is the phenomenon of mobile devices. In 2006 we were searching for ways to monitor the use of home computers by children. Today, we're searching for ways to control the use of mobile devices by our children: smartphones, video iPods, iPads, and other tablets.

A staggering 50 percent of children eight to twelve years old report that they have two or more mobile devices. Nearly one in five children eight- to twelve-year-olds (19 percent) say they have three or more mobile devices. Children report spending approximately two to three hours per day using their mobile devices. One-third of children report they would rather go without their summer vacation than give up their mobile devices.[32]

It might not come as a surprise that mobile devices have become mini-pacifiers/babysitters for many wee ones: 52 percent of all children eight and younger have a mobile device. Among the parents of these children, 29 percent have downloaded applications specifically for their children to use on phones. You may see them in restaurants or in doctor's offices: a parent with a squirmy young one who is handed her mom or dad's phone to stay occupied—and quiet.[33]

A study conducted by the Pew Research Center showcased the continuing trends of teens using text messaging as their primary means of communication. Sixty-three percent of all teens said they exchanged text messages on a daily basis. The report notes, "This far surpasses the frequency with which they pick other forms of *daily* communication, including phone calling by cell phone (39 percent do that with others every day), face-to-face socializing outside of school (35 percent), social network site messaging (29 percent), instant messaging (22 percent), talking on landlines (19 percent) and emailing (6 percent)."[34]

The volume of texting among teens has risen from fifty texts a day in 2009 to sixty texts for the median teen text user, with older girls logging more than one hundred texts in one day.[35] Even with their obsessive use of texting, teens do recognize the downsides. One-third of teens admit texting takes away from time they could be spending with friends face-to-face. Forty-four percent agree that using social media distracts them from the people they are with in person.

Teens are texting in class, in groups of other teens, at the dinner table, at work, in church, and while adults are talking to them face-to-face. We can't blame the kids—adults are texting in groups of other adults, at the dinner table, at work, in church, walking down the street, and while their teenagers are talking to them face-to-face. But it doesn't have to be that way.

A dear friend of mine became disgusted with himself and his lack of interaction with his wife and children. Without making an announcement, he walked into his home one evening and dropped his cell phone in a basket by the door. It stayed there till the next morning. (Quite a contrast from his old habit of keeping his phone in front of him until bedtime.)

He asked his son if he needed help with his math homework. He asked his older daughter if she had a minute to talk when she finished her phone call. His younger daughter put down her game and joined him in the kitchen when he chipped in to help his wife prepare salads.

One by one, his wife and teenagers started doing the same thing. All the electronic gadgets sat in the basket, at least through dinner. Now, instead of staring at their screens, the family members look at one another as they share the events of their days.

Putting your phone in a basket at home is a great start. Looking for sources of help is another.

What's a Parent to Do?

THE MOBILE TECHNOLOGY AGE IS here. We may not be able to control the industry, but we can do a better job of not allowing it to control our lives. Susan Murray, assistant professor of behavioral sciences at Andrews University, offers this perspective:

> A culture of disrespect is part of a "co-violent" society, one that celebrates mayhem while simultaneously condemning it. While violence and the media are inevitable, exposing ourselves to the negative aspects of it over and over reinforces the disrespectful aspects of our society. It is penetrating the hard-wiring of our children's psyches.[36]

As Ms. Murray reminds us, the messages of our society are confusing. We both use media and forbid it in the same day. We must do our best to send a consistent message to our children that technology has its place in helping us as long as we do not allow it to hurt us.

CTIA-The Wireless Association® and The Wireless Foundation launched the Growing Wireless campaign and website (www .GrowingWireless.com) to provide parents with tools and information to educate ourselves so we can teach our kids how to use wireless technology safely. GrowingWireless.com offers easy-to-understand information and tips for parents on how to handle issues such as cyber-bullying, sexting, and privacy. You will also find up-to-date reports on the latest wireless safety issues.[37] I encourage you to spend some time on the site and to utilize many of the tools available to help you develop a good parental management plan to protect your kids.

But even careful monitoring and screening won't be enough if we aren't practicing what we preach. You can never protect your kids from the entertainment you take pleasure in. Are you still with me?

One thing you can bank on with children ages two to nineteen is that they know us—their parents—better than we know ourselves. They see straight through our deceptions.

Parents, we helped create this disrespectful world. We can't keep blaming everyone else, including the media. If we truly want to protect our children, we must start by turning our backs on the smut. It's not okay for pornographic magazines to be in your home with adolescents milling around. It's not okay for you to spend more time online than in line with your kids at the snowball stand or the movies (yes, there are still great movies being made). It's not okay for you to text, e-mail, and surf the Web during dinner or conversations with your family. It's not okay to expect your children to adhere to higher standards than you hold for yourself.

We all need to apply that great line from Uncle Ben to Peter Parker (a.k.a. Spider Man), "With great power comes great responsibility." Come to think of it . . . get a hold of the *Spider-Man* movie series and watch it with your family in the next few weeks. You'll find a great study guide for discussion with your teens at this link:

http://www.christianbook.com/spider-and-teen-version-word-document/christianity-today-international/pd/1753DF

The guide helps you to teach your children how to discern the message behind the story in movies.

If we want to raise respectful children in this disrespectful world, our children need to see us combat the disrespectful culture rather than be a part of it.

Protecting Your Treasure

IN THE LAST TWO CHAPTERS we've taken a long, hard look at the disrespectful messages in our culture, from magazines and books to movies and the Internet. I know many days you feel helpless to combat the messages of sex for sale on every bookshelf and magazine rack. Practically any button you press on the radio or TV can lead to trouble. Images and words filled with sexual innuendo appear from cyberspace in front of your child's innocent eyes. Billions of dollars are spent by the industry to influence your children. But . . .

You can do something about it, right now. First, in your home. Give your family something better than all the entertainment that's not good for them. Give them entertainment that nourishes their souls. An afternoon unplugged in the backyard. A day in the woods, hiking and picnicking. Sharing stories of your childhood when the sun goes down, instead of turning on the television. Show your children there's a whole world to explore and learn about outside the confines of a box.

Now, you're ready to take on the giants.

Remember: David slew Goliath with a single stone. Like David, you just need to make certain you prepare for the battle. Read the account from 1 Samuel 17:34–37, when David convinced Saul he was capable of handling the giant:

David said to Saul, "Your servant has been keeping his father's sheep. When a lion or a bear came and carried off a sheep from the flock, I went after it, struck it and rescued the sheep from its mouth. When it turned on me, I seized it by its hair, struck it and killed it. Your servant has killed both the lion and the bear; this uncircumcised Philistine will be like one of them, because he has defied the armies of the living God. The Lord who delivered me from the paw of the lion and the paw of the bear will deliver me from the hand of this Philistine."

Saul said to David, "Go, and the Lord be with you."

If David could defeat Goliath, you can defeat the entertainment industry. "Go, and the Lord be with you."

David was willing to do whatever was necessary to protect his sheep. Are you willing to do whatever is necessary to protect your children, regardless of what anyone else is doing or not doing? For the sake of your children, I hope you're nodding your head.

10

Engage; Don't Entertain

LOOK, DAD, WE CAN SEE the stars!" shouted Jonathan after the roof flew off the Cunninghams' home during a tornado in the middle of the night.

Just minutes earlier, Dad had abruptly awakened Jonathan and his little sister when the alarm in town sounded, signaling trouble was coming. They rushed to the bathroom in the center of the house with Dad pulling the mattresses from their beds behind them. Jonathan and his little sister, Sara, climbed in the tub while Dad placed a mattress over their heads to protect them from the threat of falling debris. Mom and Dad huddled near the tub with the other mattress resting on their shoulders as they waited out the storm.

All was quiet now and Jonathan's mind was on the beautiful night sky. "I've never seen the Big Dipper. Can you find it, Dad?"

"Well, son, let's see," Dad answered, forgetting for a moment that they were peering through a gaping hole in their roof. "I haven't looked at the stars in a very long time. I think if we find the brightest star in the sky, we'll find the Big Dipper."

"Isn't there a Little Dipper?" Sara asked. "I want to see the Little Dipper."

For the next half-hour questions kept coming. Is there really a man in the moon? Does the sun hide the moon or does the moon hide the sun? How come we don't fall off the earth? Did God send the tornado? And on and on and on. For the rest of the night, they watched the sky as the clouds passed by. By sunrise, they had concocted a story of a family who traveled the world in a bathtub!

Two weeks later the electricity was finally restored, but this young family wasn't in a hurry to return to their old life. They liked the new life of telling stories and watching the sky. They were no longer four people living under the same roof; they were a family. A real family. Laughing together. Crying together. And most of all, playing together. Their home may have been torn apart by the storm, but their family was put back together. Their old habit of being attached to their electronic devices was replaced with a new habit of being attached to one another.

You don't have to wait for a storm to blow the roof off your home to have a night under the stars with your children. You can do it now, tonight, this weekend. I encourage you to put down the gadgets, look your kids in their eyes, and ask them to play with you before they ask you to play with them.

In this chapter, you'll find practical suggestions for how to unlock the imaginations of your children to help them soar above the storm. In the process, you'll learn how to engage with your children rather than entertain them.

* * *

TEACHERS WERE ASTONISHED, AND I was thrilled, to see the transformation that took place during a first-time visit to an elementary school for at-risk children. When storytelling time arrived, I began by asking the children to "watch" the story with their imaginations. Before I could begin, a hand flew up. "Miss Jill, wait . . . I don't know how to do that!"

"You listen with your ears, and you look with your heart," I said as I knelt down with one hand behind my ear and the other pointing to the little girl's heart. "Do you understand?"

She shook her head from side to side.

I continued, looking at all the children, "Let's practice. Close your eyes for a minute. Imagine playing on the playground with your friends. Can you see it?" All the children nodded affirmatively, including the little girl.

"Well, that's watching with the eyes of your heart. You're not looking out the window at the playground; you're using your imagination to see the picture in your head. When you use your imagination, you're looking at the world through the eyes of your heart."

I then told the children a story called "Trouble with a Capital P," a tale I wrote about twin raccoons, Peter and Penelope, who get into big trouble when they break the rules. Their all-knowing and fearless mentor, Wise Ol' Wilbur, told Peter and Penelope they could throw the baseball back and forth as long as they didn't throw it beyond their backyard. They got carried away, and consequently, their neighbor, Mrs. McDonald, ended up with a broken window because of their disobedience.

During the telling of the tale, I repeatedly asked, "Do you see?" I enjoyed watching the kids as they "watched" the story. Their heads moved from side to side as if standing on the edge of the backyard as Peter and Penelope threw the ball back and forth. By the time Peter threw the ball over Penelope's head and into Mrs. McDonald's window, all the children gasped because they "heard" the glass shatter.

When Mrs. McDonald came to Peter and Penelope's house, the children "saw" the baseball in Mrs. McDonald's hand. At the conclusion of the story, our raccoon friends helped Mrs. McDonald with chores at her home to repay her for the broken window. When I asked, "What do you think Mrs. McDonald brought to our little friends when they finished doing her chores?"

The precious little girl who didn't know she had an imagination answered, "Oh, *look*, she made them homemade cookies. What a nice lady!"

I winked at the teachers, who were grinning in amazement, as I hugged the little girl.

Imagination Is More than Knowledge

IT IS IN OUR IMAGINATIONS that problems are solved and inventions are created. It is in our imaginations that dreams meet reality, that the impossible becomes possible. A great "imaginer," Napoleon Hill, used his imagination to find his way from a one-room cabin in the hills of Virginia in the late 1800s to become our country's first great motivational speaker. He knew the value of imagination: "First comes thought; then organization of that thought, into ideas and plans; then transformation of those plans into reality. The beginning, as you will observe, is in your imagination."[1]

Webster's defines *imagination* as "the act of forming a mental image of something not present to the senses; creative ability; resourcefulness."[2] I think of imagination as the ability to look at the world with the eyes of your heart.

If we want our children to cure the diseases of the world one day or to create an invention that cuts our utility bills in half or to find a way to make this disrespectful world wholesome again, we must unlock their hearts. You hold the keys that will unlock those hearts. That's why you must be willing to expend the energy, time, and effort to engage your children's imaginations, rather than just offering entertainment to pacify their boredom.

One of the greatest "imaginers" of all time, Albert Einstein, once said, "Imagination is more important than knowledge. For knowledge is limited to all we now know and understand, while imagination embraces the entire world and all there ever will be to know and understand."[3]

If we want our children to become all they were created to be, we must engage their imaginations. Yes, it takes knowledge to win a game of *Star Wars Battlefront II* on an Xbox and skill to build a science project, but it is through imagination that the game was created and the design of the science project was conceived.

Children aren't born with knowledge, but they are born with an abundance of imagination. Observe your kids at play. Action figures aren't plastic dolls in the hands of six-year-old boys; they are superheroes saving the world, with "Kid General" in charge. When nine-year-old Beth puts Barbie in her pink convertible, they're off to meet Ken. Today Barbie's a famous rock star; tomorrow she'll be in the kitchen baking cookies. Yesterday she was at the beach with her little sisters, Kelly and Skipper. Don't tell these children this is fantasy . . . they'll tell you it's real!

It breaks my heart that children don't know how to use their imaginations anymore. We've robbed them of opportunities to do so. Rather than engaging children's imaginations with thought-provoking activities, we entertain them with mindless amusements.

Get Unplugged

WHEN WE SURVEYED A GROUP of children and asked them, "Which do you like better: video or computer games, television and movies . . . or sports and board games? Would you rather be plugged in or unplugged?" one child replied: "I like video games; they make my mind stop. I don't think when I play them, so I don't get tired. If I'm playing outside or playing those other kind of games, I have to think too hard."

This boy just happened to prefer video games, but he could have been talking about television and movies as well. Here's my point: when children are plugged in to electronic games, gizmos, and gadgets, they are unplugged from life. They're not using their imaginations; they don't have to, the box thinks for them. Think about the time your children spend in front of a box. Rather than engaging minds and senses, the box disengages minds and desensitizes emotions. It is our duty to help our children reach their full potential, which will never happen if they spend 90 percent of their time sitting in front of a box.

To **open** the mind, you must **unlock** the heart.

—Wise Ol' Wilbur

Remember the adage "Necessity is the mother of invention"? You and your kids will be forced to become creative with meals, entertainment, and lighting if you will take a Saturday to unplug for real. Take this seriously. Unplug the oven. Unplug the phone. Unplug the television and computer. Unplug the lights. Unplug *all* your electrical cords. (And no batteries allowed!)

When the sun goes down, gather your family, light a candle or two, and share stories from your childhood with your children. Sing a camp song. Play Go Fish or Pick Up Stix or Barrel of Monkeys. When was the last time you built a house of cards?

Try it—I think you'll find your kids will love "roughing it" and that the experience will bring you closer together, because you have to work as a team to figure out how to make do without electricity.

Being plugged in keeps us from plugging in to one another. I saw this in 2005 after Hurricane Katrina came through our city. The day after the storm, we had no electricity. Our neighbors were out in the street, not assessing damage, but visiting with one an-

other. But as soon as the electricity came back on, the streets emp-
tied and folks returned to their remote controls.

I realize, of course, that we can't live our lives completely unplugged. It's okay when kids use the computer for research or to chat
with friends using instant messaging, and even to play games that
have some redeeming quality—but we must help them find a balance. Apart from schoolwork, I believe the balance should be 75 percent unplugged and 25 percent plugged in. If you want your children
to engage their imaginations and use more than 10 percent of their
brainpower, don't allow them to be plugged in more than fifteen
minutes out of every hour.

Turn off the boxes, and turn them on to something better: real
life!

The rest of this chapter is going to explore ways we parents can
engage our children's imaginations by:

+ Providing opportunities for creative play

+ Being a kid with kids

+ Getting plugged in to reading

+ Celebrating the joy of having real fun

Provide Opportunities for Creative Play

WITH HIS ORDINARY VOICE, UNASSUMING personality, and gentle
manner, Fred McFeely Rogers penetrated the hearts of his viewers
on *Mr. Rogers' Neighborhood*. Despite his quiet demeanor, his love
came through loud and clear. He knew exactly what children needed,
and he provided it: the Neighborhood of Make Believe, where children used their imaginations and creativity. Mr. Rogers engaged his

young audience in play, not entertainment, because he believed in the value of creativity:

> Play does seem to open up another part of the mind that is always there, but that, since childhood, may have become closed off and hard to reach. When we treat children's play as seriously as it deserves, we are helping them feel the joy that's to be found in the creative spirit. We're helping ourselves stay in touch with that spirit too. It's the things we play with and the people who help us play that make a great difference in our lives.

I couldn't agree more. When we give our kids opportunities to be creative in how they play, we enhance their ability to do creative problem-solving as they mature.

Here are some ways you can help your kids engage their imaginations through creative play:

Make an Imagination Station

MY FAVORITE CHRISTMAS GIFT AS a child was a giant cardboard activity box that looked like a snow-covered chimney. It was filled with crayons, books, spools of yarn, scissors, and assorted "stuff" that was just stuff—until my imagination began to run wild with ideas to turn the stuff into something special.

You can get your children's creative juices flowing by gathering supplies and creating an Imagination Station. It could be a corner of the den or playroom or part of a bedroom. You don't have to teach your kids how to create something from nothing; they can teach *you* if you provide them with the opportunity to be creative. I've never known a child who had to be coerced into creating.

What do you need for the Imagination Station? One or two of

those gigantic plastic storage containers work great, because not only can they store the supplies, but your child can also use the top as a work surface, if space is tight. Don't throw away old containers from the kitchen, such as gallon jugs, oatmeal boxes, spice jars, odd-size empty boxes, and so on. Put them in your Imagination Station. Toss in some old magazines, along with some ordinary art supplies: glue, scissors, construction paper, felt, foam sheets, buttons, pipe cleaners, yarn, markers, crayons, modeling clay, and anything else you can think of. Don't forget old grown-up clothes for dress-up.

Before you know it, your kids are:

+ Turning oatmeal boxes into space rockets

+ Using photos from old magazines to illustrate original stories

+ Molding clay into creatures-come-to-life from their imaginations

+ Transforming odd-size boxes joined with pipe cleaners into trains that can transport the clay creatures

+ Turning old clothes into costumes they will use in an original play about their heroes

+ Creating funny farm animals out of empty milk cartons and a little yarn, felt, scissors, and glue

The Imagination Station encourages your children to create, not vegetate. It engages their minds and even their hearts as they concoct original stories and plays. You'll be amazed at how peacefully most children play when they're using their imagination. There's no competition between the kids, no tug-of-war, just excitement as they find the satisfaction of creating something from nothing with their own two hands.

When your kids have driven you crazy with their productions, pull out the games.

Play Games Together

INVITE YOUR NEIGHBORS, YOUR CHILDREN'S grandparents, and friends to come over one Saturday with their favorite games, favorite homemade dessert, and a card table. If weather permits, set up the tables outdoors, creating an old-fashioned carnival atmosphere. Pull out your favorite board games, and have a good time together.

If your gathering contains kids of varying ages, you might find the following list of age-appropriate games and activities helpful:

Three- to nine-year-olds: crayons and coloring books, Chutes and Ladders, Candy Land, wooden blocks, and DUPLO.

Ten- to twelve-year-olds: Silly Putty, Barrel of Monkeys, card games, TinkerToys, Lincoln Logs, Jacks, marbles, and LEGOs.

Teenagers: Dominoes, checkers, Scrabble, Clue, Life, Monopoly, and Sorry.

Don't limit yourself to table games; consider action games too. Ask your kids to come up with a list of games for all ages to enjoy together—sack race, three-legged race, relay, football toss, Frisbee, and so on—or play charades among families.

Game days provide great opportunities for the "old folks" to teach the young kids a thing or two, so get out those old board games from the attic, or scour some antiques shops for old games. Children will find out in a hurry that even though seniors aren't experts at computer games, they can play a mean game of checkers or dominoes. Encourage the teenagers to join in too. And don't be surprised if this becomes an annual event in your neighborhood.

When the weather doesn't permit outdoor play, move the playground indoors.

Turn Your Kitchen into a Playground

WE MOVED FROM A NEIGHBORHOOD with backyards to a thirty-six-story high-rise in Manhattan when the boys were four. I learned more about engaging children than I ever wanted to know. Talk about having to be creative! I decided to turn my kitchen into a playground for several hours each day.

Chad and Boyce loved it. I selected one bottom drawer and told them it was their drawer. They could play with anything they found in the drawer. In order to keep them interested, I frequently changed the contents of the drawer, filling it with things such as Tupperware, lids from my

---

Classic Toys

Here's a list of twenty-four classic toys that are just as engaging today as the day they first came out, and even better, no electricity or batteries are needed—just your child's imagination and you.

Play-Doh

Jump rope

Matchbox cars

Airplanes

Fire trucks

Yo-yos

Mr. Potato Head

Bubbles

Building blocks

Super Balls

Candy Land

Mousetrap

Bingo

Checkers

Slinky

Silly Putty

Model cars

Science sets

Monopoly

Weebles

Radio Flyer wagons

Dollhouses

LEGOs

Kites

pots and pans, wooden spoons, plastic bowls and utensils, and mea-suring spoons. To grown-ups, my kitchen looked like the utilitarian center of the house, but through the eyes of my little boys, it was their indoor playground.

I didn't have an indoor playground when I grew up, but there *was* a special place set aside for a special activity . . .

Work Jigsaw Puzzles Together

WHEN I WAS GROWING UP, my father had a brown card table in the corner of the den with a puzzle-in-progress on it. Most nights after supper, Daddy would excuse himself from the dinner table "to think awhile in my corner." We knew what that meant—Daddy was going to work on a jigsaw puzzle—a complex one, at that. Even though he rarely extended a formal invitation, the rest of us understood we were always welcome at his table.

My father's interest in puzzles extended far beyond the chal-lenge he found on the card table. "The tougher the puzzle, the harder you have to think," he would say when questioned about the inten-sity he gave his hobby. "It's about more than working a jigsaw puzzle. It's about solving everyday puzzles."

It was delightful to watch him dig with great patience through the box of a thousand cardboard cutouts, searching for the right piece. He would grumble during the search and then say, "Aha!" when he found the missing piece.

During my teen years if I needed to talk to Daddy, I often joined him at the card table after supper. I chose to talk when he was at the card table because I didn't have to look my father in the eyes if the subject was unpleasant! We enjoyed many good conver-sations at the puzzle table, but that wasn't the only benefit. As I watched my father work on the puzzles, I also learned how to approach life's problems: assess the situation, work through the options, and keep working at it until you solve the problem.

Don't wait any longer to set up a puzzle table at your house. You'll all learn a lot about solving problems—as a family.

Another sweet memory I have of my father is the times he became the human monkey bar. A virile man with great strength, he would stand erect with his arms bent at 90-degree angles and allow us to swing back and forth on his "bars." He enjoyed being a big kid.

Be a Kid with Your Kids

WITH ALL THE PRESSURES OF adulthood, we often lose the pleasures of childhood. Do yourself a favor, and delight your children by being a kid in some small way. As silly as this may seem, you'll earn more respect from your children when you're willing to just enjoy being a kid with them than from telling them about the big deal you closed at the office. It's as simple as the ABCs:

Always smile—Do this especially when you don't feel like it.

Blow bubbles—Walk in the house with a bottle of bubbles in hand.

Color in a coloring book—Do this rather than read one night.

Draw a self-portrait—Let the children put *your* picture on the refrigerator.

Eat a peanut butter and jelly sandwich—Invite the kids to the table for a surprise supper.

Finger paint—Yes, use your fingers, not brushes.

Goofy faces—See who can make the funniest face.

Hide-and-Seek—Ask your kids to play before they ask you.

Ice-cream cones for everybody—See who can eat one without getting a brain freeze.

Jump rope—Learn the Double Dutch.

Kick a can down the street with your kids—Challenge the kids to a contest.

Look up—Watch the stars at night and the clouds during the day.

Musical chairs—Rearrange the chairs after supper, and turn on the music.

No TV—Don't turn on the TV. Just don't do it!

Old-fashioned hopscotch—Draw the game board on the driveway and start hopping.

Paper airplanes—Challenge the kids to a contest.

Questions—Ask silly, silly questions.

Race around the block—Challenge the kids, even with the neighbors watching.

Scissors, Rock, Paper—Use this game to determine who goes first in the next board game.

Take a walk with the family—Walk hand-in-hand without your watch on your wrist.

Uncontrollable laughter—Start giggling for no apparent reason. Your kids will join you.

Ventriloquism—Try it; it's not as hard as it seems.

Walk barefoot in the grass—Go back to your childhood, or experience something new!

Xylophone—Kids love this instrument.

Yodel—Try it; this *is* as hard as it seems.

Zoo animal sounds—Heard a chimpanzee lately? Neither have your kids.

I must confess, I'm really just a nine-year-old kid, at least in my heart. My friends used to compliment me on being such a great mom, because I would get in the middle of whatever activity the boys were doing. Most of the time I just smiled and said, "I try."

But, just between you and me, I'll tell you the truth: I wasn't being a gallant, unselfish mom; I was participating out of total selfishness. I miss being a kid! Why, just yesterday I joined in a football game with my godson and his friends. They couldn't believe this "old lady" could throw a pass!

My heart jumps for joy when I look out my front window and see the neighborhood boys playing ball in my front yard. I don't care if the ball lands in the flowers or even if they break a window. The flowers can be replanted and the glass replaced. I'm just thrilled to see those boys unplugged and plugged in to real fun.

Plug in to Reading

DO YOUR CHILDREN HAVE A difficult time reading? Do they tend to put off their reading? Let me share a few suggestions to encourage your children to read:

+ Keep books with you at all times. Waiting in a doctor's office is a great opportunity to read.

✦ Set aside a time in the evening for reading. Mom and Dad, stop your activities and read too. Show your children that reading every day is important.

✦ Do some research with your kids about the authors of the books they are reading. If your children know about the life of the author, they'll enjoy the books even more.

✦ Make a special place for reading—a quiet corner with good lighting and comfortable seating. (When I was a child, my favorite reading spot was a mimosa tree in our front yard. The limbs were strong and spread apart enough to make an inviting seat to relax and enjoy a good book.)

✦ Read to your children, even when they're old enough to read to themselves. Show how much fun reading can be. Make the characters of a book come alive with innovative voices and gestures.

✦ For every hour your children read, allow them to stay up an extra thirty minutes on Friday and Saturday nights.

✦ Reward the completion of their school's summer reading list with a trip to the bookstore. Allow your child to select a book of his choice, when the "have-to-read" books are finished!

When the reading is done, it's time to get back to those activities that seem unimportant to you but mean everything to your children.

Celebrate the Joy of Having Real Fun

MY MOTHER ALWAYS SAID, "YOU find time to do the things you really want to do." How true! If you don't subscribe to that thought, I can assure you that your children do. So, since childhood passes quickly, make the most of these years by celebrating the joy of having real fun with your children. Give them your undivided attention, unplug from the busyness, and engage your kids in conversation.

You have an opportunity to love your kids and stimulate their imaginations today. Give hugs in abundance, get in the kitchen and bake a batch of cookies, pull out the box of "stuff," and spend time doing fun, simple things with them. Your children need more of the little things and less of the big things, because the little things really are the big things.

A Family That Did It

WILMER AND BETSY MILLS WERE agricultural missionaries in remote parts of Brazil for almost nine years while their four children were growing up. Their house was equipped with an electric generator that pumped water to the house and gave them four hours of electricity at night. There was no telephone, air conditioning, computer, or television, although they did have a record player and a stack of old Walt Disney records. There was no shopping mall or playground, but the children were never bored; they never complained about having nothing to do. According to Betsy, "The children invented their own fun." They grew up bilingual, learning English and Portuguese simultaneously.

Days were filled with creative activities. Jenny and Kate loved to decorate dollhouses, built from rough board crates by their father. They spent three to four hours a day drawing in notebooks, a few hours working on their studies and the rest of the daylight hours playing store outside with their Brazilian friends, who lived in mud-and-stick huts. John grew up as the neighborhood mascot, surrounded by his siblings' activities, enjoying cooking in the kitchen and playing with baby jungle monkeys. Wil, as the oldest, enjoyed more freedom to roam with his friends, fishing in the river and hunting iguanas with his handmade slingshot.

Reading books was a favorite ritual for the kids—an hour in the morning and afternoon accompanied nap times. Many nights they were read to for more than two hours. The children learned to read for themselves at young ages and developed exceptional comprehension skills. They were fortunate to be a part of a readers' service for missionaries, which sent boxes of children's books twice a year. Family favorites were the Bobbsey Twins books, *Encyclopedia Brown*, *The Great Brain*, *The Hobbit*, and the *Little House on the Prairie* series. *The Lord of the Rings* and *The Chronicles of Narnia* were read aloud twice! The children enjoyed visualizing what they read and soon invented their own adventure series, illustrated in notebooks that rivaled C. S. Lewis's and J.R.R. Tolkien's works.

The children learned to play rhythm instruments, the guitar, and piano. A nightly routine often included singing four-part harmony in Portuguese as a family. Every night the family enjoyed devotions of prayer and Bible stories.

All four children are now married with their own young children, and each has excelled in various creative fields. John loves woodworking and singing, and is an award-winning cook. Jenny plays the Celtic harp and does portraiture. Kate has a master's in painting and has been a college art professor. Wil writes music, and is an accomplished brick-oven bread baker and a well-known poet. I recently listened to Wil read from his latest book of poetry at a prestigious book festival. The imagery of his words tapped the imaginations of his listeners as he shared the thoughts of his soul. Just as the room filled with heavy emotion, he picked up his guitar to amuse us with a humorous song. After receiving rousing applause, he was forced to linger well beyond his time allotment in order to answer questions from aspiring poets and to enjoy accolades from his admirers.

Listening to Wil share his poetry and entertain his audience has become a sweet memory. Wil passed to heaven in 2011 at the age of forty-one. A line from his obituary said it all: "Wil was a renaissance man who pursued all things Godly, true, and beautiful, and who shared those things as well as himself generously with others." Wil became all God intended him to be. His work made an impact on our world. His life left an imprint on our hearts.

If you ask Betsy the secret of the phenomenal creative success of her children, she quickly says it was the blessing of the "Brazilian Wild West." Betsy says with great humility, "The kids engaged themselves. I wasn't the teacher, but the facilitator. I provided the supplies—pens, paper, paints, empty boxes, books, musical instruments. It was my great joy to sit back and watch my children tap into their imaginations. I was always astounded by the depth of creativity they found within themselves. My children had no choice but to use their imaginations to the fullest." Much to Betsy and Wilmer's credit, too, the Mills "kids" have become part of that unique group of individuals who tap into more than 10 percent of the brain's capacity.

We can learn a great lesson from the Mills family. Preparing our children to be productive members of society is not to be found in the electronic gadgets of the new millennium but in the simple pleasures of engagement. Nights spent gathered as a family, not around the television but around the table, playing games or making music. Saturdays romping in the backyard, playing leapfrog and eating ice cream. Sunday afternoons painting the next great masterpiece on butcher paper with poster paints.

Looking at the world through the eyes of our children enriches our lives and reaches their hearts. You must unlock the hearts of your children to open their minds.

11

Teach Gratefulness, Not Greediness

THE HOUR AFTER the storm has passed is indescribable. The winds are calm. The air is quiet. The hum of electricity is gone. Gradually, the sun returns to its rightful place in the sky. Neighbors come to the street to assess the damage. The early-dawn freight train colliding with itself turned out to be a two-hundred-year-old oak tree crashing through the roof of your next-door neighbor's house. Your lot is covered in limbs and debris. Uprooted trees and roof shingles dot the yard, but your home is secure.

But your dear friends next door? Before you can get to them, they're coming to you to see if you're all right. Really? Their home is shredded. Their treasures are destroyed, and they're worried about *you*. Having lost all they hold dear but each other, they want to be certain everyone else survived too.

You might think you're the one filled with more gratitude than your neighbor, but gratitude doesn't work that way. It really doesn't matter that their things are gone. Your neighbors are grateful to be alive.

Surviving a serious storm changes you. Perspectives change. Priorities change. The little things become the big things, and the big things don't matter so much anymore. What matters is that you're alive and have another chance at living, at giving.

A friend who lost his home in Hurricane Gustav said, "Stuff is just that, stuff." His family spent their days after the storm helping others. They rebuilt their home, but they didn't fill it up again with "stuff." Four years later, this family finds more joy in giving than in getting. They discovered the secret to a heart of gratitude—give, give, give.

Is it possible to instill this kind of gratitude in your children? The buying power of today's teens is out of control. In 2011, 25.6 million teenagers in the United States spent more than $200 billion. And what did they buy? Clothing was number one, followed closely by entertainment, including movies, videos, and CDs.[1]

I wonder how much "stuff" they gave away? I wonder how grateful they were for what they had?

The difficult truth is that teens are filling up, but still empty. In more than one research study, teens were found to feel significantly more isolated, misunderstood, and emotionally sensitive or unstable than in decades past. Teens were also more likely to be narcissistic, have low self-control, and express feelings of worry, sadness, and dissatisfaction with life.[2] They can't develop gratitude if they don't learn how to give.

In this chapter, you will learn how to keep your children from drowning under the weight of too much stuff by replacing the wrong stuff with the right stuff. Even in this age of indulgence, your children can develop gratitude rather than greediness.

Even the greatest candy store in the world can't satisfy the heart longings of children.

✳ ✳ ✳

HAVE YOU EVER SAT UNDER a lamppost that resembled a giant chocolate kiss? Unless you've visited "The Sweetest Place on Earth," I doubt you've seen such a sight. When you cross the city limits of Hershey, Pennsylvania, there's something to delight the senses at every turn.

It's Candy Land come to life.

On a recent visit, I wandered into Hershey's Chocolate World to see the story behind the making of chocolate. Inside, I was greeted with row upon row of candy, treats, toys, and stuffed animals of every description. Just as I decided that this was truly the land of enchantment, the magical spell was broken by a child's ear-piercing "Gimme! Gimme!" and her tired parents' "Enough! Enough!"

In the midst of this sweet paradise, I felt disheartened to see a child who was so discontent. And worse, the more she received, the more she wanted. This little girl was in the middle of Candy Land, but she could not be satisfied.

Unfortunately, she has plenty of company.

Living in Candy Land

OUR COUNTRY HAS BECOME CANDY Land, hasn't it? Land of the free (deal) and home of the brave (shopper). Look around. We are the consumer giant, devouring every fad that comes along as if our lives depended on it. Without the latest, greatest, fastest, biggest, loudest, newest gadget, we act as if we've become nobodies. We're working longer hours than ever before to make more money so we can buy more things, even though we have no time to enjoy the things we already have, not to mention a place to store them.

We all know someone who just bought a new car with the latest thingamabob, someone who just purchased a new home in the trendiest subdivision, or someone who's always on the cutting edge of fashion. We're bombarded with more than three hundred thousand commercials per year on television and three million on the radio.[3] Add to that the ads in print media—magazines, newspapers, and books. As we drive on the freeways, we see more ads on billboards, in neon lights, and on the sides of trucks and buses.

We cannot escape the inundation of advertising—others telling us what we "need" in order to be somebody—that enters our consciousness and lodges in our subconscious, shaping our desires and wants, and deceiving us into thinking we really do need whatever it is they're selling. And so we buy.

"Everybody has too much stuff. It's the American way," said a manager of a climate-controlled storage building.[4] In an article for the Baton Rouge, LA, newspaper, *The Advocate,* John Austin reports, "The insatiable race for space is fueling a $15 billion self-storage industry that dwarfs Hollywood's annual $9 billion. What was once a mom-and-pop business has become an industry with companies whose stock is traded on the New York Stock Exchange."[5]

I wonder, *Are those storage units filled with things people need? Or are they filled with things people want?* Why do we wonder that our kids want so much, when our own wants are out of control? Could it be we're passing our greediness on to our children?

Scripture reminds us: "What good is it for a man to gain the whole world, yet forfeit his soul? Or what can a man give in exchange for his soul?"[6] We're literally selling out, and I'm afraid it's our children's hearts and souls that we're losing in the exchange. What are we teaching our kids through our own buying habits and through the things we purchase for them?

Filled, Yet Still Empty

IF YOUR CHILDREN ARE GROWING up in Candy Land, with their every whim granted, they'll never develop hearts of gratitude. They'll spend their lives wanting more, while missing the simple, everyday pleasures.

In Chapter 2, I talked about how our kids come into our lives with empty hearts needing to be filled. When we attempt to fill those hearts with "stuff" rather than our time, our children continue to want more, because for every emotional need that's unmet, their emptiness grows deeper. A child with an empty heart has a hard time being grateful. It's not the child's fault.

Ungratefulness is epidemic among children today because parents have:

+ Offered unwarranted praise, which leads children to expect rather than accept

+ Given children things instead of themselves and their time

+ Given too much and expected too little

When your children begin to expect "things" from you, they lose their gratitude. Think of the daughter whose father travels frequently for his job. Because Dad feels guilty for being away, he brings his daughter a gift as a token of his love. But as time passes, she stops anticipating her father's return and, instead, anticipates the gift he will bring her. When the day comes that Dad doesn't bring a gift, the daughter is unhappy—with life and with her father. Parents who overindulge their kids are nurturing ungratefulness in their children's hearts. The more things these parents give, the more things their kids want.

I witnessed this firsthand recently while visiting a friend. When the doorbell rang one morning, the three-year-old went crazy, running to the door screaming, "Nana's here! Nana's here!" Before Nana could get in the door, the little girl was pulling Nana's purse off her arm. Nana tried to calm her, saying, "Let me get in the door, then we'll look in my purse."

But the little-girl-gone-wild couldn't wait. She kept pulling. Nana's purse strap snapped and the purse crashed to the ground. Still unstoppable, the little girl started digging through the purse to find the treat Nana surely had brought her. When she didn't find anything that looked like a treat to her eyes, she left the broken purse and all its contents in the doorway to go back to her old life. No "Hi, Nana" or remorse for breaking her purse.

I never did see the little girl give her grandmother a hug.

Is there a way to fill those empty hearts with the "right" stuff?

I believe there is!

It will take hard work, but it can be done. Cultivating a grateful heart takes time and intentional, not accidental, parenting. You must make a concerted effort to give opportunities for your children to develop gratitude. You'll need commitment, perseverance, and a bit of creativity, but you can do it!

Cultivating a Heart of Gratitude

AS WE DISCUSSED EARLIER, WE need to enroll our children in the School of Respect as soon as they come into this world. If our goal is to fill our children's hearts with respect for God and others, and we succeed, our kids will grow up with grateful hearts that are focused on others and not self.

With that in mind, here are some ways to help your kids develop grateful hearts:

Train Them in Manners

DEFINED BY AN ATTITUDE OF the heart that's self-giving, not self-serving, manners are much more than memorizing a set of rules. When we teach our children to be well mannered, we are teaching them to focus on *others*, and on how *others* feel and what *others* need. Manners help kids to grow up believing *It's more about others and less about me.* So:

TYKES: Three to Five

+ Encourage your kids to show concern for others. Give them a few pennies to share whenever someone asks. Drop a coin in the charity box at McDonald's. Buy an extra canned good for the food pantry, and let your child place it in the barrel.

+ Say "thank you" to your kids, and gently, consistently remind them to do the same. It's better to say, "What do you need to say?" than "Say thank you."

+ Say a prayer with your kids the next time you hear a siren or see an emergency. Show them how to think outside themselves by praying for others in need.

+ Watch for opportunities to teach service. Even young children can open car doors for the elderly or befriend the child who's left out by others.

+ Teach your children how to say grace before meals.

+ Begin to work on their table manners. Brush up on your own table manners, because your children are emulating every move you make. Start with holding utensils properly.

✦ Expect "Yes, Ma'am" and "Yes, Sir." Such words teach respect for elders. Don't allow your children to call adults by their first names. You need to establish the boundary between child and adult.

TWEENS: Six to Twelve

✦ Teach telephone etiquette: how to answer the phone, take messages, and make calls.

✦ Expect tweens to clean their rooms and bathroom without your assistance.

✦ Require them to write thank-you notes, even when all they did was spend the night at a friend's house.

✦ Teach your son to take a flower with his gift to a girl's birthday party.

✦ Insist that boys open doors for ladies and seat them for dinner.

✦ Teach girls how to graciously accept help from a gentleman.

✦ Accept no back talk. Use a respectful tone of voice with your children, and expect the same from them.

✦ Have your children practice a handshake with a firm grip while looking the recipient in the eyes.

✦ Begin work on the details of table manners: serving

from the left and removing from the right, no reaching, asking for food to be passed to you, waiting for all to be served before you begin eating, not leaving the table until all are finished, and asking to be excused before rising.

+ Ask your tweens to serve adult guests.

+ Teach them to say "excuse me" when appropriate.

+ Look for ways to involve them in service—helping the elderly, helping a younger child, helping Mom.

+ Refer to *Manners of the Heart at Home* for more help in working with your children.

TEENS: Thirteen to Nineteen

+ Invite adults over for dinner, and involve your teens in your conversations.

+ Remind teens not to go to a friend's house without calling first.

+ Teach teens to offer to help serve and clean up when eating at a friend's house.

+ Encourage teens to write a thank-you note for a meal or an overnight visit at a friend's house.

+ Model being quick to say "I'm sorry" and being slow to criticize.

+ Teach them that their dress tells others what they think of themselves.

✦ Teach your sons to be respectful of girls—to:

1. Open car doors for them

2. Seat their dates for dinner

3. Not walk in front of a girl in public places, such as restaurants and theaters, but walk beside her or behind her

4. Not use inappropriate language or tell off-color jokes

✦ Teach your girls how to be ladies—to:

1. Sit modestly

2. Never use foul language, at all, ever

3. Never pursue a boy

4. Allow boys to treat them like ladies

✦ Teach the importance of responding to an RSVP invitation within twenty-four hours of receipt.

✦ Above all, insist that commitments be kept.

If you work on your child's manners with consistency and firmness, your child's heart will likely swell with gratefulness. When kids are grateful, they have positive attitudes and are ready to serve others rather than themselves. Grateful children grow into respectful young adults.

Of course, it's one thing to insist that your children use respectful, grateful, well-mannered speech and quite another to cultivate the attitude behind those actions. Well-groomed children who know the rules of etiquette can also be devious little troublemakers if they have been taught to "put on their manners" to impress others rather than use manners to make the lives of those around them more pleasant.

That's where the ideas in the rest of this section can help.

> Those who have good *hearts* find pleasure in being unselfish. For he who does a kindness to another does a greater kindness to himself.
>
> —Johnny Gruelle, "The Kind Hearted Ginger Bread Man"

Allow Your Kids to Have a Sense of Ownership

AN OLD PAINT BUCKET SAT in the cabinet under the kitchen sink in my childhood home. It wasn't a leftover from the last painting job; my parents had placed it there to teach us a valuable lesson in gratitude. Taped to the side of the bucket was the word *vacation*, reminding us of its purpose. Our annual summer vacation was determined by the amount of change tossed into the bucket during the year. Every time one of us washed the dishes, we had an opportunity to make a contribution to our family's vacation fund. We understood we could make a difference in the choice of destination by how much we sacrificed during the year. The year Disney World opened in Florida, my brothers and sisters and I did extra chores for months so we could put enough money in the bucket to go there on our family vacation.

I remember that vacation well—and the sense of satisfaction and gratitude I felt, in part because I had helped my family make this dream trip possible. Even though the ride in the car was long, we kids didn't argue (well, maybe just a little!). When we got there, we didn't complain about it being too hot or too cold, or being too tired, or that the lines were too long. Each of us had worked hard to earn this vacation, so we appreciated it. We weren't going to ruin "our" vacation.

Here's the unexpected twist: Our parents gave each of us a little spending money when we arrived. Sound counterproductive? It wasn't. We'd had the privilege of helping to pay for the vacation. In turn, we were given a gift of grace from our parents for our enjoyment, just because they loved us!

You can use this same principle of offering ownership with clothing, movies, and any form of "extras." For instance:

+ If your daughter finds a jacket at the mall she "must have," insist that she earn the money to pay for it. If she makes a concerted effort, offer to help out with part of the cost.

+ Buy movie tickets for your kids, but let them earn the money for popcorn.

+ Give each child a specific area of responsibility in the care of the home. Your son might be in charge of the trash. If he doesn't do his job, don't do it for him. Leaving the job to him will give him ownership of that duty. If he won't be home the night before garbage pickup, he's responsible for getting a substitute to do his job. Or your daughter could be in charge of cleaning the hall bathroom. The same rule applies—if she can't do it, she's responsible for getting a replacement. When the kids know that if they don't do their jobs, the jobs won't get done, they appreciate their home and feel an important part of it—they take ownership.

Teach Them that Good Things Come to Those Who Wait

I WANTED TO HELP WHEN I saw a young mother with a tired two-year-old and a five-year-old pleading for a candy bar at the grocery store. But I knew there was little I could do to make her life easier at that moment. As I watched this desperate mother struggling to maintain her composure, I wanted to encourage her to say no to her child's pleas for a treat.

If we want to instill gratefulness in our children, we can't give in when they plead with us for a treat or present. When we do, we are rewarding them for begging. Kids who get what they want when they want it grow up to be ungrateful, impatient adults. How much better if they could learn early on that good things come to those who wait![7]

Ideally, parents need to teach this lesson before their kids even go to school, but kids can learn this when they are older too. It works like this. Simply inform your kids that you won't be buying them any treats when you go to the grocery store or mall. Each time they ask for something, say no—and stand by it in the checkout line.

I know how difficult this is, but you can win this battle if you will stay calm and lower your voice rather than raise it as the tension mounts. Each time a child's voice is raised, lower yours, until you reach a whisper—no matter how loud the bellowing. The howling will stop because your child has to hear what you're saying. If this has been an area of struggle for you, don't give up. With persistence, you can win this battle. I cannot tell you how long it will take before your child stops begging; that depends on how long your child has had the upper hand. But I can assure you that if you will stand firm, you can cure this problem.

Once you have taken back this territory, occasionally offer your kids a treat when you're out shopping. This teaches them that "good things come to those who wait" and that whining is of no benefit.

Help Them Experience the Joy of Giving

YOU CAN TAKE THIS A step further by helping your kids experience the joy of giving. When you offer your child candy, place a few coins in his hand to purchase a treat to give to a friend or a sibling at home.

This simple act of benevolence will bring your child joy and can help her develop a deep desire to share with friends and siblings. This is the secret to developing a heart of gratitude—the satisfaction of giving rather than getting. Kids who learn this secret will have their focus on others rather than self, and they will grow up with self-respect.

> Count that day lost whose low descending sun, Views from thy hand no **worthy** action done.
>
> —From a framed embroidery piece, 1803

Model Gratefulness

PARENTS WHO HAVE GRATEFUL HEARTS don't have to work hard to instill gratitude in their children's hearts. They simply live what they teach. It flows naturally, if you truly believe what you're teaching.

So how do we model gratefulness for our children? Here are some ways:

+ Show love and appreciation to your spouse. Say "thank you" for small kindnesses. Insist that the children respect your spouse.

+ When you are contemplating a purchase, ask if the item is really something you (or a family member) need or if the item is something you simply want. In general, if the item is a want, you shouldn't buy it.

+ Don't complain about minor annoyances or about wanting things you don't have.

+ Say "thank you" to your children.

+ Thank service providers—from clerks to bank tellers to the paper courier to those in the military.

+ Show appreciation for simple pleasures: good health, creation, kindness, a good night's rest, a good meal.

+ Send your child a written thank-you for an exceptional task completed.

+ Display good manners.

We had just moved from New York City back to the South and the sweltering summer heat. Boxes were piled everywhere. Nothing in our temporary home had found its place yet. I was grateful to have found the box of sheets and pillows before nightfall. As the boys and I knelt by their beds, one of the boys opened our prayer time: "Now, bow your heads. Thank you, God, for Mom's smile. Thank you, God, for my brother's funny face [strange thing to say since they're identical twins!]. Thank you, God, for Dad. Thank you, God, for New York City. Thank you, God, for Louisiana. Thank you, God, for trees. Thank you, God, for grass. Thank you, God, for my new tennis shoes. Thank you, God . . ." and on and on and on. After quite a long dissertation, he said, "Excuse me, God, a minute—Mom, did I forget anything?"

You know what? He didn't forget a thing. Not because he counted his blessings one by one, but because he came to our Father with a grateful heart. It had been a long, miserable day. I'm sure that's why my son was grateful for my smile. There were many moments when I wanted to scream. I did lose my cool at one point in the 100-degree weather, but my sweet son chose to forget the bad moment and remember the good.

I often share with young moms the lesson I learned from my son that day: On the bad days, remember the good days. On the good days, forget the bad days. Children can do it, so why can't we? We can learn a lot about gratefulness from observing young children. They're grateful for the little things—"the sun and the moon and the stars above." They notice when we're smiling and when we're not. And at the end of the day, they can always find something to be grateful for.

Proverbs reminds us that "a happy heart makes the face cheerful, but heartache crushes the spirit."[8] Do you want to instill gratefulness in your children? Remove any bitterness in your own heart, and your heart of gratitude will flood over into the hearts of your children.

Smile . . . just smile, and your children will smile back.

Ten Simple Ideas for Instilling Gratitude

1. Encourage the simple pleasures. Make gifts for each other. Play games rather than renting a movie. Spend the night in the backyard as an adventure at home.

2. Teach money management. Make sure each of your children has a piggy bank and is required to save a portion of his or her allowance. In addition to an allowance, let your children do extra chores for money to be used for "wants" they purchase themselves.

3. Start a tradition of adopting a family (or neighbor) throughout the year. Provide a meal you prepare and deliver together.

4. Do not allow whining. The best cure for whining is to ignore it totally.

5. Don't allow idleness. Don't let your tweens and older kids sit around doing nothing. Put them to work—outside the home and inside the home. A little hard work does wonders to change an attitude of ingratitude.

6. Get outside with the family. Enjoy God's creation. Appreciate the beauty. Bring back a sense of wonder that the chaos of everyday living takes away.

7. Pray with your children on bended knee each night.

8. Help your children memorize Philippians 4:8: "Finally, brothers, whatever is true, whatever is noble, whatever is right, whatever is pure, whatever is lovely, whatever is admirable— if anything is excellent or praiseworthy—think about such things."

9. Give love and appreciation for a job well done rather than buying a treat.

10. Give your child age-appropriate responsibilities. Nothing builds a child's self-respect like being held accountable for chores and decisions. Don't nag, but expect the best from your child, and you'll probably get it.

12

Listen to the Children

During the weeks following Katrina, more than five thousand homeless men, women, and children found a welcoming place at the River Center in downtown Baton Rouge with hot food, soft beds, and respite from the multitude of decisions to be made. The staff of Manners of the Heart spent many hours with the children to give them momentary distractions from their circumstances.

The hopelessness in the eyes of the adults and the terror in the eyes of the children made it impossible to serve without tears. I cried on the way down, and I cried on the way back, for I had a home, not just a building, where I could sleep at night.

One fateful day, I felt a tug at my skirt as I stood in the middle of a crowd of children. When I looked down, a precious child with arms reaching to the heavens pleaded, "Hug me, hug me, hug me." (Not "pick me up" or "hold me," as little ones so often say, but "hug me.")

When I lifted this child to my chest, she wrapped her arms around my neck and her legs around my body. Her head fell on my shoulder as she squeezed the breath out of me. After a moment she pulled back and began rocking from side to side. With those legs wrapped all the more tightly around my waist, she brushed the sweaty bangs across my brow, then squeezed my face between her tiny hands. "Will you stay with me?" she asked. Looking in those big brown eyes starving for love, I muttered, "I will."

Children were brought in and out of an area set aside for our program throughout the day. It was ironic that I wasn't staying with her, she was staying with me, glued to my side, absorbing every word and observing every action. She stayed as long as she was allowed. Then, in an instant, she disappeared as quickly as she had appeared.

> **Arise**, cry out in the night,
> as the watches of the night begin;
> pour out your heart like water
> in the presence of the Lord.
> Lift up your hands to him for
> the lives of your children.
> —Lamentations 2:19

The following day I discovered the little girl was part of a group of "misplaced" children. "Children of the storm," I tenderly called them—children alone, stripped from their parents. No wonder she was desperately clinging to me. I never saw her again, but I can still feel those tiny hands squeezing my face, and I can still hear her words, "Will you stay with me?"

I see the same hopelessness in many parents today. And I see terror in the eyes of children. Parents dazed by the thousands upon thousands of decisions imposed upon them by our narcissistic culture. Parents inundated with disrespect in the workplace, in the neighborhood, and within their own families. Children who need parents to protect them and prepare them.

Oh, tired and weary parents, will you stay with your children? Will you see them through the storm? Will you fortify their souls to withstand the storm surges of our culture?

We have to get this right for the sake of the children. For the sake of children everywhere. Won't you listen to their pleas?

* * *

DURING THE SUMMER OF 2005, Manners of the Heart volunteers interviewed more than four hundred children between the ages of four and fourteen for our "Listen to the Children" study. The children represented a cross section of kids from our community.

My interest in conducting this study was inspired by a book written in the seventies by Dr. Kenneth Chafin, *Is There a Family in the House?* Dr. Chafin interviewed one hundred children and asked the following ten questions, which we included in our survey:

1. What's a family?

2. Who is in your family?

3. Why do you think we live in families?

4. What would it be like if people did not live in families?

5. What are mothers like? What are fathers like?

6. What are mothers for? What do they do?

7. What are fathers for? What do they do?

8. Who is the most important person in your family to you?

9. If you could change one thing in your family, what would you change?

10. What does your family do together for fun?

To Dr. Chafin's questions, we added ten of our own:

1. Who is your hero?

2. What's the nicest thing your parents could ever tell you?

3. Are your parents always busy?

4. What's more important . . . being smart or being nice?

5. Do you do chores at home? If you don't do them, what happens?

6. Which do you like better—playing board games, sports, and outdoor stuff; or TV, movies, and video games?

7. Do your parents watch a lot of TV?

8. Do you like to read? Do/did your parents read to you?

9. When your parents tell you to do something, do you usually listen?

10. Have you ever watched PG-13 and/or R-rated movies?

We discovered, much to our surprise, that today's children responded to the questions about family just as those interviewed thirty years ago. Even though the culture has changed, the understanding of the way things should be hasn't changed. Kids seem to know instinctively what a family should be.

What's a family?

✦ "A group of people who love each other."

✦ "A group of people who never go away."

✦ "A mommy and daddy and brothers and sisters."

+ "A man and a woman who marry and have babies to-gether."

+ "A mommy and daddy who love each other forever."

+ "People who teach you right from wrong."

+ "People who tie your shoes."

+ "A mommy and daddy who help you when you're hurt."

+ "A mom and dad who teach you how to be a mom and dad."

+ "People who don't laugh at you."

+ "People who play together."

+ "You have to have a family, or you can't live."

What are mothers and fathers like?

+ "Fathers are like big hammers. They pound people if they mess with their children."

+ "Mothers are like 'a cherry on an ice-cream sundae.' Fathers are like 'the cone underneath the ice cream.'"

+ "Mothers are your bestest friend."

What's more important, being smart or being nice?

+ "I want to be smart, because then I would know to be nice."

+ "If you're not nice, then you're not smart."

+ "I know I'm smart, because I try to be nice."

+ Ninety-six percent responded without hesitation, "Nice."

Children know the truth, but no one is listening. It's we adults who have gotten confused about what's right and what's wrong. We're the ones who have lost our way.

Children come into the world needing guidance to become all they were created to be. They need direction. They need examples to follow. They need someone to nurture their souls and protect their hearts. They need someone who will offer real answers. They need someone to walk beside them every step of the way with encouragement. They need more than the outside world has to offer.

They need parents who will parent.

Bitter are the tears of a child;

Sweeten them.

Deep are the **thoughts** of a child;

Quiet them.

Sharp is the grief of a child;

Take it from him.

Soft is the heart of a child;

Do nothing to harden it.

—Lady Pamela Glenconner, 1916

We can't blame the media or Hollywood or the schools or the government or all the other institutions in the world for the way our children are turning out. They make our job much more difficult, but they are not to blame. We are. God doesn't entrust His children to the world, but to parents.

In the movie *Kramer vs. Kramer*, Dustin Hoffman plays a workaholic father, Ted Kramer, whose wife, Joanna, makes a tragic decision to leave not only her husband but also their son. Here's a man who hasn't a clue how to be a father with a young son and an all-consuming career, but he's willing to learn. Joanna resurfaces, asking for custody. When Ted refuses, they wind up in a bitter battle. The most telling scene in the movie is when Ted testifies in court with great intensity that he's reduced his workload because raising a child requires so much time simply to listen.

In a moving monologue, Ted looks from the jury to the judge to his former wife and asks, "What is it that makes somebody a good parent?"

He answers his own question as he continues, "It has to do with constancy. It has to do with patience. It has to do with listening to them. Pretending to listen to them when you can't even listen anymore."[1]

Of all the skills we need in order to raise respectful children in this disrespectful world, the skill of listening outweighs all the rest. Listen to God's leading, listen to your heart, and listen to your children.

When you do your part, God will take care of the rest.

Final Word

THE WIND OF destruction has been blowing since the beginning of time. In the first garden, Adam and Eve succumbed to the serpent's lie that God was trying to deny them pleasure. Can't you see the wind blowing through the tree as the apple was eaten? We all know the consequences brought about by yielding to that temptation.

The wind kept blowing.

Hundreds of years later, the apostle Paul warned the Romans in 2:8, "For those who are *self-seeking* and who reject the truth and follow evil, there will be wrath and anger" (emphasis added). The Romans didn't listen. We know what happened to the Roman Empire.

Blow, wind, blow.

Move forward to the tenth century when vainglory, evident in boastful royalty and those who bragged of adventures not taken, became the mantra of the day. An Old English poem by the same name compared the two opposites of human conduct: on one hand, the proud man and on the other hand, the virtuous man. Soon the proud man fell to his enemies, while the virtuous man prevailed.

Blow, wind, blow.

In the 1960s we were told we *needed* self-esteem. We were told to love ourselves so others would love us. Rather than recognizing that self-esteem was just a new name for an old sin, we fell for the lie just as Adam and Eve had done in Eden. And we've been paying the price ever since.

Blow, wind, blow.

In the aftermath of destruction, there is hope. The light of truth has burst through the darkness. From psychologists to social workers. From preachers to teachers. From grandparents to parents. We're no longer fooled by the lie. We now know the truth: self-esteem is the cause of our problems, not the solution.

We can't afford to continue raising our children by the standards of this disrespectful world. You've read the statistics; you know the devastation. You may have picked up this book because you're living in the eye of the storm.

Let me help you help your children. It all begins with you and the choices you make when you put down this book. Walk through the chapters with me from another perspective. In His Word, God says:

+ Raise your children with eternity in mind. (Deuteronomy 32: 46)

+ He will satisfy your soul questions so you can answer your children's soul questions. (Psalm 34:4, 5)

+ He will give you His purpose for your life so you can thrive in this world, not just survive. In turn, you can help your children find His purpose for their lives. Don't worry so much about how they perform, but who they become. (Proverbs 19:21)

+ Praise Him in the morning, praise Him at noontime, praise Him when the sun goes down. In the act of praising Him, you'll find encouragement when you grow weary. Teach your children to praise Him rather than looking for praise in the world. He will honor you both. (Isaiah 25:1)

+ He gives you boundaries to keep you safe. Accept His discipline for your good. Have no fear of punishment . . . He took care of that for you. Give your children boundaries to keep them safe. Discipline for their good, not yours. (Deuteronomy 5:29)

+ Gratitude flows from a contented heart. God promises to meet our needs, not our wants, but our needs. We should do the same for our children. (Luke 12:15 and Mark 8:36)

+ And, finally, listen. I know, but I must say it again, listen to the Lord. And then listen to your children. (Proverbs 2:1–5)

Noah listened at a time when no one else was listening. He followed God's instructions without hesitation and without adding his own ideas. He saved his family from impending disaster. They rode out the storm in the safety of the ark. When the flooding of the earth ceased, God remembered Noah:

And he sent a wind over the earth, and the waters receded . . . At the end of the hundred and fifty days the water had gone down . . . and the ark came to rest . . . The waters continued to recede until the tenth month, and on the first day of the tenth month the tops of the mountains became visible.

After forty days Noah opened the window he had made in the ark and sent out a raven, and it kept flying back and forth until the water had dried up from the earth . . . He . . . sent out the dove from the ark. When the dove returned to him in the evening, there in its beak was a freshly plucked olive leaf! . . . He waited seven more days and sent the dove out again, but this time it did not return to him . . .

Noah then removed the covering from the ark . . . Then God said to Noah, "Come out of the ark . . ." Noah came out, together with his wife and his sons' wives. All the animals and all the creatures that move along the ground and all the birds—everything that moves on the earth—came out of the ark, one kind after another.

Then Noah built an altar to the Lord . . . The Lord . . . said in his heart . . . "As long as the earth endures, seedtime and harvest, cold and heat, summer and winter, day and night will never cease."

Then God blessed Noah and his sons and established a covenant with them, saying . . . "I have set my rainbow in the clouds, and it will be the sign of the covenant between me and the earth. Whenever I bring clouds over the earth and the rainbow appears in the clouds, I will remember my covenant between me and you and all living creatures of every kind."

You can be a modern-day Noah. Listen to God's instructions for survival. Keep your family close. Your home can become an ark of safety for your children. Your home can become the safe haven. He'll guide you as you guide your family through the tumultuous waters of this culture.

Do it God's way. Noah did. And look what happened to his family.

They survived the storm.

Small Group Study Guide

Parent. /'par-ent/N

Dwell on the ramifications of that word for a minute or two. Not mother or father, grandmother or grandfather, but *parent*. I can't think of a more important title in life than this one.

Guardian. Protector. Nurturer. So much more than the dictionary definition: "one that begets or brings forth offspring."[1]

The question isn't whether or not you're a parent. You *are* a parent. The question is whether or not you will *parent*. /'par-ent/ *v*

Train. Teach. Coach. Guide. Lead. Interestingly, the dictionary lists parent as not only a noun, but also a verb, giving us a great reminder that it isn't enough to *be* parents, we must know *how* to parent. Maybe we weren't parented well. Maybe our lives are so busy, we don't have time to parent. Maybe . . . you fill in the blank.

You're reading this because you have a deep desire to raise children who will leave a positive mark on the world. You want to raise children who will be respectful in their youth and become respectable in adulthood.

You *can* do it. You *must* do it. The children being born today can become the Rebuilder generation of tomorrow—if we do our jobs as parents, guardians, and grandparents. We can turn the tide on disrespectfulness, entitlement, and narcissism.

My hope is that this study guide will enable your small group to encourage each other, hold each other accountable, and find strength in numbers as you make decisions about how you will raise your children.

This guide is designed for a seven-week study.

Chapter Grouping

Session One

CHAPTER 1: What Went Wrong?

Session Two

CHAPTER 2: Where Have All the Parents Gone?

CHAPTER 3: Enroll in the School of Respect

Session Three

CHAPTER 4: Stress Purpose, Not Performance

CHAPTER 5: Coach; Don't Cheerlead

Session Four

CHAPTER 6: Set Boundaries Without Building Walls

CHAPTER 7: Use Discipline, Not Punishment

Session Five

CHAPTER 8: Shield Your Treasures from the Trash: *Magazines, Books, and Music*

CHAPTER 9: Shield Your Treasures from the Trash: *Movies, TV, Video Games, and the Internet*

Session Six

CHAPTER 10: Engage; Don't Entertain

CHAPTER 11: Teach Gratefulness, Not Greediness

Session Seven

CHAPTER 12: Listen to the Children

Session Divisions

SCRIPTURE: Foundation from God's Word

READING ASSIGNMENT: Chapters of the book covered in the lesson

LESSON OBJECTIVE: The take-away from the lesson

MATERIALS: Extra supplies, books, props, etc.

YESTERDAY: Reflection questions based on your childhood experiences. Recognizing how we were parented helps us to understand why we parent the way we do. We can discern constructive and destructive ways to parent our children.

TODAY: Activities and discussion questions centered on your present-day family's experiences

TOMORROW: Heartwork for the home to help reinforce good habits, create new habits, and change not-so-good habits

PRAYER: Prayer for the coming week

PARENT PAUSE: Lighthearted moment for reflection

Sample Session

Each group is unique and will have its own ideas and desires for the group. Here is a sample of how an hour-and-a-half meeting could be structured to make the most of your time together.

>*10 minutes:* Meet and greet as folks are coming in. Snacks and drinks are wonderful, but not essential. This is an opportunity to get to know one another better.

>*5 minutes:* Introductions. Allow all members to introduce themselves or, as the weeks continue, to welcome new guests. Remind participants that all discussions remain confidential among group members.

5 minutes: Opening prayer time.

15 minutes: Discuss the heartwork (from the TOMORROW section) from the previous week, offering each other suggestions and help from experience. Discuss the answers to YESTERDAY's questions to enable reflection on where parenting decisions come from in your present family.

45 minutes: Activities and discussion of TODAY's suggestions and questions. Challenge for TOMORROW's questions and suggestions.

10 minutes: Closing prayer time. E-mail prayer requests to the group the following day, so that members can pray for one another during the week. Close prayer time by reciting the prayer for the week in unison.

One last suggestion: if you missed the movie *Secretariat,* I encourage you to see it. AJ Michalka's theme song, "It's Who You Are," is a great summation of one of the goals of this study: to help you help your children discover who God created them to be. The words of this song put it all in perspective. It can be found on YouTube at http://www.youtube.com/watch?v=kShUvrr7QVU.

Enjoy . . . Parents who have great kids usually have kids who have great parents. May each and every one of you become a great parent with great kids!

SMALL GROUP SESSION ONE

CHAPTER 1: *What Went Wrong?*

But the fruit of the Spirit is love, joy, peace, patience, kindness, goodness, faithfulness, gentleness, and self-control: against such there is no law. Those who belong to Christ Jesus have crucified the sinful nature with its passions and desires. Since we live by the Spirit, let us keep in step with the Spirit. Let us not be desirous of vainglory [self-esteem], provoking one another and envying one another.

—Galatians 5: 22–26 (a combination of NIV and KJV)

LESSON OBJECTIVE: Choosing self-esteem or self-respect as your parenting goal

READING ASSIGNMENT: Preface, Introduction, and Chapter 1; Galatians 5:16–26

MATERIALS: Mirrors—one for each two participants. (8" x 10" mirrors are available at Dollar Tree)

YESTERDAY

Think back to your childhood . . .

+ How has our society changed? Are we more respectful or more disrespectful? More selfish or less selfish?

+ What do you believe caused the changes?

TODAY

Ask your participants to sit in pairs facing each other. One person from each pair needs to hold a mirror in front of his/her face. Ask the following questions:

Who do you see when you look in the mirror?

 ✦ *My reflection*

 ✦ *I can see people behind me in the mirror.*

Who do you not see when you look in the mirror?

 ✦ *The person sitting across from me*

 ✦ *Anyone in front of me*

In the mirror, you see only yourself and people behind you. You cannot see those in front of you. You see only where you have come from. You cannot see where you're going. In the mirror, you cannot see God, and you cannot see God looking at you.

But what if you put the mirror down and stood at a window? Would you see yourself in the window?

 ✦ *You would still see yourself, but a transparent image.*

 ✦ *You would see through yourself, past yourself.*

What would you see?

 ✦ *You would see others.*

 ✦ *You would see where you're going.*

 ✦ *You would see the possibilities of what could be.*

When we raise our children in the mirror, they become lost in themselves.

They can be at either one extreme or the other . . . either self-conceited or self-conscious. Life becomes all about what the world will do for them.

When we raise children at the window, they can see others. They can see the possibilities before them. They can find their place in the world. Life becomes all about what they will do for the world.

Our children follow where we lead . . . to the window or to the mirror.

Questions for discussion:

1. Are you living in the mirror or the window?

2. Are your children respectful? Why or why not?

3. Are good manners important to you? For your children? Why or why not?

TOMORROW

Heartwork for Home

1. Are you living in the mirror or the window?

2. Which category best describes your current parenting style?

   a. Befriending your kids

   b. Letting your kids make their own decisions

   c. Never refusing your children anything

   d. Training your children's hearts

3. Are you trying to develop self-esteem or self-respect in your children?

4. Do you insist that your children use the following?

   a. "Yes, Ma'am" and "No, Sir"

   b. "May I get your chair?"

   c. "Excuse me."

   d. "I'm sorry."

5. Are you praying regularly for wisdom to raise your children to be respectful? If not, begin today.

PRAYER

Father,
Open the eyes of my heart to see Your truth.
Enable me to become the parent You need me to be
so that I can raise my children to become all You created them to be.
Through Your Son, Amen.

PARENT PAUSE

A teacher asked her students what each wanted to become when they grew up. A chorus of responses came from all over the room.

"A football player." "A doctor." "An astronaut." "The president." "A fireman." "A teacher." "A race car driver."

Everyone had an answer except Tommy. The teacher noticed that he was sitting quietly and still. So she said to him, "Tommy, what do you want to be when you grow up?"

"Possible," Tommy replied.

"Possible?" asked the teacher.

"Yes," Tommy said. "My mom is always telling me I'm impossible. So when I get to be big, I want to be possible."[2]

SMALL GROUP SESSION TWO

CHAPTER 2: *Where Have All the Parents Gone?*
CHAPTER 3: *Enroll in the School of Respect*

Therefore, since we have been justified through faith, we have peace with God through our Lord Jesus Christ, through whom we have gained access by faith into this grace in which we now stand. And we boast in the hope of the glory of God. Not only so, but we also glory in our sufferings, because we know that suffering produces perseverance; perseverance, character; and character, hope. And hope does not put us to shame, because God's love has been poured out into our hearts through the Holy Spirit, who has been given to us.

—Romans 5: 2–5

LESSON OBJECTIVE: Choosing the parenting style that enables your family to graduate from the School of Respect

READING ASSIGNMENT: Chapters 2 and 3; Romans 5:1–5

MATERIALS: Chart paper

YESTERDAY

Think back to your childhood . . .

+ Were you raised by child-centered, parent-centered, or character-centered parents?

+ Were your soul questions answered?

TODAY

Discuss the heartwork from the past week.

Draw an outline of a heart on chart paper. Ask the question from page 31: Today, you have the opportunity to fill your child's empty heart. What will you place in that heart? Fill in the heart with the answers.

The answers that are given become the character traits we want to help our children cultivate.

Draw the School of Respect chart from page 38 and discuss ways to answer the soul questions of the children represented in your group.

Questions for discussion:

1. List the four most important aspects of character-centered parenting from pages 26–28. Discuss how well you are doing in each area.

2. Using the list on page 29 as a challenge, admit an area of weakness and ask for accountability as you work to improve.

3. Have you set family goals you can share with others?

TOMORROW

Heartwork for Home

Chapter 2: *Where Have All the Parents Gone?*

1. Which category of parenting best describes you?

   a. Parent-centered

   b. Child-centered

   c. Character-centered

2. Are your expectations for your children attainable?

3. What motivations are behind your dreams and aspirations for your children?

4. Do you sometimes find yourself pressuring your children to achieve a certain "success"?

5. Do you spend a lot of time and effort developing character in your children?

6. Have you made the firm decision that, no matter what, you will do your best to raise respectful children in this disrespectful world?

7. Are you optimistic, doubtful, or pessimistic about your decision? Why?

8. How does your list of priorities compare to the one on page 29?

Chapter 3: *Enroll in the School of Respect*

1. What is more valuable to you, your children's character or their grades?

2. Are you working to answer your children's soul questions in each stage of the School of Respect?

3. Do you sometimes brush your children off when they're trying to get your attention, especially when you're too busy? How do you think they interpret this?

4. Are duties around the house just something to do (an option), or are they necessary responsibilities for your children as members of the family?

5. If your children viewed God's love through you, would it be unconditional, patient, always trusting, and slow to anger (1 Corinthians 13: 4–7)? What did they see in you last week?

6. In the past, has your "no" meant an absolute "no," "sometimes," "maybe," "it depends," or even "yes"?

7. Are you giving your children opportunities to serve others?

8. Have you been attempting to demand respect from your children rather than commanding respect from them? Are you ready to change your ways if needed?

PRAYER

Father,
I pray that each of my children would grow
in wisdom and stature and favor with You and man.
Enable me to parent with eternity in mind so that I can satisfy
the answers to my children's soul questions, according to Your will.
Through Your Son, Amen

PARENT PAUSE

The man in the supermarket was pushing a cart that contained, among other things, a screaming baby. As the man proceeded along the aisles, he kept repeating softly, "Keep calm, George. Don't get excited, George. Don't get excited, George. Don't yell, George."

A lady watching with admiration said to the man, "You are certainly to be commended for your patience in trying to quiet little George."

"Lady," he declared, "I'm George."

SMALL GROUP SESSION THREE

CHAPTER 4: *Stress Purpose, Not Performance*
CHAPTER 5: *Coach; Don't Cheerlead*

For in this hope we were saved. But hope that is seen is no hope at all. Who hopes for what they already have? But if we hope for what we do not yet have, we wait for it patiently. In the same way, the Spirit helps us in our weakness. We do not know what we ought to pray for, but the Spirit himself intercedes for us through wordless groans. And He who searches our hearts knows the mind of the Spirit, because the Spirit intercedes for God's people in accordance with the will of God. And we know that in all things God works for the good of those who love Him, who have been called according to His purpose.

—Romans 8: 24–28

LESSON OBJECTIVE: Coaching to help your children find God's purpose for their lives.

READING ASSIGNMENT: Chapters 4 and 5; Romans 8: 24–28

MATERIALS: Chart paper

YESTERDAY

Think back to your childhood . . .

✦ Were you parented or pushed to achieve?

✦ Did you receive false praise or genuine encourage-ment as a child?

TODAY

Discuss the heartwork from the past week.

Use the chart paper to list the warning signs of perfectionism, the differences between praise and encouragement, and three ways to build character in children.

Questions for discussion:

1. Using the section on perfectionism, discuss the dam-age of perfectionism and how to keep your children from becoming self-defeating perfectionists.

2. Praise and encouragement are two very different par-enting techniques. Discuss the difference and which offers the greater opportunity for helping your chil-dren become all they are meant to be.

3. What are three ways you can help your children de-velop character, starting today?

TOMORROW

Heartwork for Home

Chapter 4: *Stress Purpose, Not Performance*

---

1. How do you deal with your child's loss in a competition?

2. Do the duties you assign your children teach them duty and responsibility?

3. Do you find it easier to give up or to stick things out?

4. Do you encourage your children to set goals?

5. Are you a perfectionist?

6. Do you push your children toward perfectionism?

7. Do you want your children to be number one or their best?

8. Do you set the following goals? In writing?

    a. Family goals

    b. Career goals

    c. Financial goals

9. Do you pray together as a family? Do your children see you praying?

10. If you're concerned that your child is headed down the path to perfectionism, use the list on pages 73–74 to

help you identify the signs. If you find yourself nodding in agreement with four or more of the indicators, make a commitment to help your child overcome this self-defeating trap by using the suggestions in the chapter as a start.

Chapter 5: *Coach; Don't Cheerlead*

1. Are you a parent who refuses to give up in spite of all odds?

2. Do you find yourself coaching—or cheering—your children?

3. Do you sometimes give false praise to your children, hoping they'll feel good about themselves?

4. Do you let your children know your expectations for them?

5. Do you tell your children the truth in love about their performances in sports or music or academics?

6. Do you offer guidance in your words and actions to help your children achieve their goals?

7. Do your priorities match Coach Landry's: God, family, football (or whatever the task at hand)?

8. If your children followed in your footsteps, would that lead them in the right direction?

9. Challenge yourself as a parent to be a coach, not a cheerleader, using the list on page 99 as a guide.

PRAYER

Father,
Guard my heart against perfectionism.
Give me words of genuine encouragement for my children.
Teach me how to be an effective coach so that I can help
my children develop character to live with purpose and hope.
In Your Son's name, Amen

PARENT PAUSE

There is nothing training cannot do. Nothing is above its reach.
It can turn bad morals to good;
it can destroy bad principles and recreate good ones;
it can lift men to angelship.

—Mark Twain

SMALL GROUP SESSION FOUR

CHAPTER 6: *Set Boundaries Without Building Walls*
CHAPTER 7: *Use Discipline, Not Punishment*

…this word of encouragement that addresses you as a father addresses his son? It says, "My son, do not make light of the Lord's discipline, and do not lose heart when He rebukes you, because the Lord disciplines the one He loves, and He chastens everyone He accepts as His son." Endure hardship as discipline; God is treating you as his children. For what children are not disciplined by their father? If you are not disciplined—and everyone undergoes discipline—then you are not legitimate, not true sons and daughters at all. Moreover, we have all had human fathers who disciplined us and we respected them for it. How much more should we submit to the Father of spirits and live! They disciplined us for a little while as they thought best; but God disciplines us for our good, in order that we may share in His holiness. No discipline seems pleasant at the time, but painful. Later on, however, it produces a harvest of righteousness and peace for those who have been trained by it.

—Hebrews 12: 5–11

LESSON OBJECTIVE: Setting boundaries without building walls through effective discipline

READING ASSIGNMENT: Chapters 6 and 7; Hebrews 12: 5–11

MATERIALS:

+ Index cards and tape or stick-it notes

+ Chart paper

YESTERDAY

Think back to your childhood ...

+ Were the "house rules" in your home negotiable? Did your parents "no" mean NO?

✦ Were there walls between you and your parents?
Are there still walls today?

✦ Were you punished or disciplined?

TODAY

Discuss the heartwork from the past week.

On index cards or stick-it notes, have each participant write actions parents take that build walls between their children and themselves. Tape each one to the chart paper, stacking as you go to create a wall. Draw a child standing next to the wall.

On June 12, 1987, President Reagan challenged Soviet leader Mikhail Gorbachev in a speech at the Brandenburg Gate near the Berlin Wall with the most famous words of his presidency. "Tear down this wall," he exhorted, as a symbol of Gorbachev's desire to increase freedom in the Eastern Bloc through glasnost (transparency).

Don't set your children up to demand that you "tear down this wall" by allowing your rules and attitude to build a wall between you. Children need your transparency. They need to know you're a fallible human being. They need to know you make mistakes. They need to know you're real. They need to know you see them and hear them. Boundaries build trust. Walls create resentment and rebellion, behind which an angry storm will brew.

On the same chart paper, make a chart of the differences between punishment and discipline. Give examples of each.

Questions for discussion:

1. Give examples of nonnegotiables.

2. List three ways to discipline from a heart of love.

3. Choose three points of preventive discipline from the lists on pages 128–136 to discuss.

TOMORROW

Heartwork for Home

Chapter 6: *Set Boundaries Without Building Walls*
---

1. Do you and your spouse always stand unified as a team?

2. Do your children clearly understand what is expected of them?

3. Do they obey without questioning or complaining?

4. Are you setting boundaries, not building walls?

5. Are you developing the necessary character traits in your children before they start elementary school?

6. Are you firmly instilling family values in your children that you hope will stay with them?

7. Are there "house rules" for your home that are nonnegotiable?

8. Do you spend focused time with your children?

9. Choose a way of staying emotionally connected to your children from the suggestions on pages 107–09. Make a commitment to add at least one connection for each child in the next month.

Chapter 7: *Use Discipline, Not Punishment*

1. When you discipline your children, are you careful to make certain the penalty fits the disobedience?

2. Do you discipline your children to punish them or to change a wrong behavior?

3. What is the motive behind your discipline?

   a. Anger

   b. Fear

   c. Love

4. Are your current disciplinary techniques effective?

5. When contemplating discipline, what are you more concerned with?

   a. Your child doing good

   b. Your child feeling good

6. Do you often yell at your children to correct them?

7. Do you find yourself correcting your children for the same things you sometimes do?

8. When you make mistakes, do you admit you're wrong and ask your child for forgiveness?

PRAYER

Father,
Grant wisdom to know the boundaries my children need
to be protected and fortified.
Give me courage to use effective discipline
so that my children develop respect for
You, others, and themselves.
In Your Son's name, Amen

PARENT PAUSE

Novelist Pearl S. Buck told her sixteen-year-old daughter she wouldn't allow her to attend a party of mixed teenagers where there would be no adult supervision. The girl wailed, "You don't trust me!" Mrs. Buck's reply was, "Of course, I don't trust you. I couldn't trust myself at sixteen, seventeen, eighteen, or as much farther as you care to go!" When you face the fact that you don't trust yourself in a situation, the only wisdom is to be careful not to put yourself into that situation.

—*Homemade*, May 1989

SMALL GROUP SESSION FIVE

CHAPTER 8: *Shield Your Treasures from the Trash:*
Magazines, Books, and Music
CHAPTER 9: *Shield Your Treasures from the Trash:*
Movies, TV, Video Games, and the Internet

Blessed are those whose ways are blameless, who walk according to the law of the Lord. Blessed are those who keep His statutes and seek Him with all their heart—they do no wrong but follow His ways. You have laid down precepts that are to be fully obeyed. Oh, that my ways were steadfast in obeying your decrees! Then I would not be put to shame when I consider all your commands. I will praise you with an upright heart as I learn your righteous laws. I will obey your decrees; do not utterly forsake me.

How can a young person stay on the path of purity? By living according to Your word. I seek You with all my heart; do not let me stray from Your commands. I have hidden Your word in my heart that I might not sin against You. Praise be to You, Lord; teach me Your decrees. With my lips I recount all the laws that come from Your mouth. I rejoice in following Your statutes as one rejoices in great riches. I meditate on Your precepts and consider Your ways. I delight in Your decrees; I will not neglect Your word.

—Psalm 119:1–16

LESSON OBJECTIVE: Protecting your children from being infected by the world, while you work to affect the world for good

READING ASSIGNMENT: Chapters 8 and 9; Psalm 119

MATERIALS: Computer for showing the "good" sites that offer help in combating the media-gone-wild

YESTERDAY

Think back to your childhood . . .

+ What was the greatest media threat to your innocence?

+ What was the worst media influence in your teenage years? Did you see and hear things that were too mature for you?

TODAY

Discuss the heartwork from the past week.

Questions for discussion:

1. Discuss your children's role models. Are they who you want them to be?

2. Are you willing to change your media choices to help your children make wise decisions about their media choices?

3. What do you believe the author meant by "The Wireless Generation"?

4. What kinds of things do you do to help influence the culture for good? Can it impact your kids to see you doing these things?

Group Challenge:

Using the list below, choose at least three suggestions you will commit to following in the next forty days. You might just bring your family out of the wilderness and back to real living! Agree to hold one another accountable in your study group.

+ Kids' bedrooms are screen-free zones.

+ No television before school.

+ All homework must be completed before using electronic media.

+ Electronic media must not be used before the sun goes down.

+ Screen time is between 6:30 and 8:30 p.m. only.

+ No electronic media is to be used during meals (including phones and TVs).

+ Electronic media must be shared and everyone must have equal amounts of time.

+ If someone does not follow the rules, that person must do the dishes.

✦ Kids must have had an hour of activity before using electronics.[3]

I'd like to offer four sources of help in combating the world of media:

✦ The Truth Project at www.truthproject.org. Outstanding training to combat the media lies in today's culture.

✦ Plugged In at www.pluggedin.com. Undisputedly, the best site for wise media discernment.

✦ *Plugged-in Parenting: How to Raise Media-Savvy Kids with Love, Not War* by Bob Waliszewski. Thorough, sensible help for handling media appropriately with your children.

✦ Please visit our website at www.mannersoftheheart.org to find "Plugged into Life"—a list of one hundred ideas for unplugging from electronics and plugging into the family.

TOMORROW

Heartwork for Home

Chapter 8: *Shield Your Treasures from the Trash:
Magazines, Books, and Music*

---

1. Do you allow your young daughter to buy teen magazines?

2. Do you know what your teenage children think about the latest entertainment (songs, magazines, books) the world is offering them?

3. Have you become blind to the destructive garbage the media is offering your children? Have you allowed your children to be filled with it?

4. Do you know what type of music your children listen to? What type of books they read?

5. Are your choices of media helping your children make wise decisions about what they read and listen to?

Chapter 9: *Shield Your Treasures from the Trash: Movies, TV, Video Games, and the Internet*

1. Do you know how many hours a week your children watch television?

2. Are you lenient about what you allow your little ones to watch?

3. Do you preview the movies your children want to watch, even those rated PG-13? Do you allow your ten- to twelve-year-old to watch PG-13 movies?

4. Do you know what your children are watching at friends' houses? Which video games they're playing?

5. Do you have safeguards in place regarding your children's use of the Internet?

6. Do the shows your children watch have a positive or negative influence on them?

7. Do you sometimes watch the very things you prohibit your children from watching?

PRAYER

Father,
Protect my children from the onslaught of filth in our culture.
Give me the courage to stand against it.
Give me the boldness to speak up
and stand up for the good and the right,
regardless of the consequences in the short term.
I want to be part of the solution, not part of the problem.
In Your Son's name, Amen

PARENT PAUSE

I like Chuck Colson's job description for parents:

Parents take small, self-centered monsters, who spend much of their time screaming defiantly and hurling peas on the carpet, and teach them to share, to wait their turn, to respect others' property. These lessons translate into respect for others, self-restraint, obedience to law—in short, into the virtues of individual character that are vital to a society's survival.

SMALL GROUP SESSION SIX

CHAPTER 10: *Engage; Don't Entertain*
CHAPTER 11: *Teach Gratefulness, Not Greediness*

Bear with each other and forgive one another if any of you has a grievance against someone. Forgive as the Lord forgave you. And over all these virtues put on love, which binds them all together in perfect unity.

Let the peace of Christ rule in your hearts, since as members of one body you were called to peace. And be thankful. Let the message of Christ dwell among you richly as you teach and admonish one another with all wisdom through psalms, hymns, and songs from the Spirit, singing to God with gratitude in your hearts. And whatever you do, whether in word or deed, do it all in the name of the Lord Jesus, giving thanks to God the Father through Him.

—Colossians 3: 8–17

LESSON OBJECTIVE: Engaging children to fill their hearts with gratitude for all things, big and small

READING ASSIGNMENT: Chapters 10 and 11; Colossians 3

MATERIALS: Chart paper

YESTERDAY

Think back to your childhood . . .

+ Did you grow up with a dad who was disengaged due to his work schedule?

+ Was service to your community and giving back part of your upbringing?

TODAY

Discuss the heartwork from the past week.

Using chart paper, list twenty-five big and small ways you and your children can serve others. Have each participant choose one or two opportunities for his or her family to consider.

Questions for discussion:

1. If you woke up one morning to realize thirty years had passed and your children were all grown up, would you regret not having done certain things with or for your children?

2. Have you been guilty of giving too much and expecting too little? Share with the group and brainstorm ways to undo the damage.

3. Share some memorable giving moments you have had with your children. What kind of activities did they involve?

Group challenge:

Look for an opportunity to serve your community as a group, such as:

+ Habitat for Humanity Build

+ Food bank

+ Soup kitchen

+ Nursing home

+ Delivering treats to neighbors, just because

+ Volunteering in public school

Chapter 10: *Engage; Don't Entertain*

1. Do you help your children exercise their imaginations? Do you often use your imagination?

2. How often do you play board games or have picnics with your family?

3. Do you have dedicated time for reading to your children?

4. Can you think of some things that you've been meaning to do with your children but have been putting off because you "haven't had any time"?

5. Can you think of the *most* memorable moments that you've shared with your children?

6. How often do you sit and listen to your children to find out what's in their hearts?

7. Will you give your children something other than an electronic device on their next birthday?

Chapter 11: *Teach Gratefulness, Not Greediness*

1. How is your heart?

 ✦ Full or empty

 ✦ Hurting or happy

 ✦ Anxious or calm

 ✦ Disturbed or peaceful

 ✦ Grateful or greedy

2. Does advertising—someone else telling us what we need—have a big influence on what you consider to be your "needs"?

3. Do you find yourself giving your children things rather than spending time with them?

4. Are you more concerned with your children's comfort or their character?

5. Do you often intentionally give opportunities to develop gratitude in your children?

6. Which philosophy do your actions teach and exhibit to your children?

 ✦ Being served

 ✦ Serving others

7. When teaching your children manners, do you emphasize the reason behind having manners? Or do you just demand them to *be nice*?

8. How are your children's hearts?

    ✦ Grateful

    ✦ Greedy

PRAYER

Father,
Do not allow me to replace entertainment for engagement.
Bring to the top of my mind ways to engage with my children
every day. Teach me how to model gratefulness
and help my children experience the joy of giving.
In Your Son's name, Amen

PARENT PAUSE

Charles Francis Adams, a nineteenth-century political figure and diplomat, kept a diary. One day he entered: "Went fishing with my son today—a day wasted."

His son, Brook Adams, also kept a diary, which is still in existence. On that same day, Brook Adams made this entry: "Went fishing with my father—the most wonderful day of my life!"

The father thought he was wasting his time while fishing with his son, but his son saw it as an investment of time.

The only way to tell the difference between wasting and

investing is to know one's ultimate purpose in life and to judge accordingly.

—Silas Shotwell, *Homemade*, September 1987

SMALL GROUP SESSION SEVEN

CHAPTER 12: *Listen to the Children*

These are the commands, decrees and laws the Lord your God directed me to teach you to observe in the land that you are crossing the Jordan to possess, so that you, your children and their children after them may fear the Lord your God as long as you live by keeping all his decrees and commands that I give you, and so that you may enjoy long life. Hear, Israel, and be careful to obey so that it may go well with you and that you may increase greatly in a land flowing with milk and honey, just as the Lord, the God of your ancestors, promised you.

Hear, O Israel: The Lord our God, the Lord is one. Love the Lord your God with all your heart and with all your soul and with all your strength. These commandments that I give you today are to be on your hearts. Impress them on your children. Talk about them when you sit at home and when you walk along the road, when you lie down and when you get up. Tie them as symbols on your hands and bind them on your foreheads. Write them on the doorframes of your houses and on your gates.

—Deuteronomy 6:1–9

LESSON OBJECTIVE: Raising respectful children who grow up to become respectable adults who love the Lord with all their hearts, with all their souls, and with all their strength, and transform this disrespectful world in His name

READING ASSIGNMENT: Chapter 12 and Final Word; Deuteronomy 6

MATERIALS: Index cards

YESTERDAY

Think back to your childhood . . .

- ✦ Did your parents listen to you?

- ✦ Did you have the kind of childhood you would like to give your children? Did you have the kind of childhood you would like to shield your children from? Either way, it's up to you today!

TODAY

Discuss the heartwork from the past week.

Questions for discussion:

1. What have you learned through this study that will change the way you parent?

2. Using the index cards, write down the changes you would like to make in your family. Keep the cards in a private place and check them as you go through the next several months as reminders of the promises you made to yourself and to God.

3. Commit to memorizing "The Family Protection Prayer" found in Appendix B of the book, as you form the habit of praying it every morning. Nothing you can do will be more important than covering yourself in the armor of God and holding the shield of faith for your children until they are ready to carry it in their own faith.

Group challenge:

Commit to continue praying for one another. How wonderful it would be to keep the group going once a month as a support group! There is strength in numbers when making parenting decisions that run countercultural. To know there is a group of parents who are praying "The Family Protection Prayer" every morning is enough to make you walk through your day with the boldness of conviction. To know you're not the only one who will not allow your twelve-year-old to attend a PG-13 movie gives you the courage to stand by your decision. To know you're not the only one who is willing to unplug on Saturdays begins to build a community that chooses to do things differently.

TOMORROW

Let me challenge you to ask your children the twenty questions found on pages 227–28. You might be surprised by their answers.

Your children came into the world needing guidance to become all they were created to be. They need direction. They need examples to follow. They need someone to nurture their souls and protect their hearts. They need you to be their parent and to parent.

You might be accused, like Noah, of being crazy in meticulously planning every detail to survive the flood no one else seems to understand is coming. Take heart from Noah's story—his family survived the flood and thrived after it!

Rest assured, I will be praying for you as you lead your family to safety.

PRAYER

Father,
I acknowledge that I cannot parent my children
without Your wisdom and Your guidance.
My deepest heart's desire is for my children
to one day call You Father.
In Your Son's name, Amen

PARENT PAUSE

Heartwork Prayer

> I pray that out of His glorious riches He may strengthen
> (your child's name) with power through His Spirit in (your
> child's name)'s inner being, so that Christ may dwell in
> (your child's name)'s heart through faith. And I pray that
> (your child's name), being rooted and established in love,
> may have power, together with all the saints, to grasp how
> wide and long and high and deep is the love of Christ,
> and to know this love that surpasses knowledge—
> that (your child's name) may be filled to the measure of all
> the fullness of God.
>
> —Ephesians 3: 16–19

Appendix A

A Personal Note to Single Parents

I'M SURE YOU'VE noted there are few personal stories from our home that include my husband. Oh, how I wish there could have been more! My husband left our home the first week of our sons' sixth-grade school year.

It was devastating.

No one on earth was more important to me than my husband, my college sweetheart. His life was my life. Together we had worked hard to achieve his goals. Just when I thought "one of these days" had finally come for us, he decided that rather than begin a new chapter in our family history book, our book needed to close. I begged him to stay; the boys begged as well, but to no avail.

I wanted you to know that this book has been written from the heart of a mom who survived the devastation of rejection and the unbearable pain of broken dreams. Having lived it, I wholeheartedly agree with Dr. James Dobson that "the most difficult job in the world is that of a single mom."

But with God's help, I've done it. I want you to know that you can do it too.

Stand with assurance before the throne. It is true that you cannot raise your children alone. But don't fret . . . you have three allies to help you—the Father, the Son, and the Holy Ghost. The Lord will bless you with an extra arsenal of protection when you're willing to allow Him to be the head of your home. Take a stand for your children, in spite of your loss and pain.

Your children can become respectful children in the midst of great disrespectfulness, if you will not allow your heart to grow bitter. Single moms or single dads, it is your own bitterness, not the actions of the wayward spouse, that will destroy your children. I know you cannot fill two roles, but you can fulfill your role. God will fill in the gaps.

Let me share a priority list with you that I lived by after my husband left home:

Priority List to Live By

God

Children

Family

Service to the church

Service to the community

The list could go on . . . with one exception. We don't belong on our own priority list.

Many days, I wondered and worried who would take care of me while I was taking care of my sons. Out of fear, I tried to put myself on my list. But God made this truth perfectly clear to me—He would take care of me, if I kept my eyes on Him. If I had put myself on my list, I would have been telling God that I could take care of myself without Him.

Scary thought . . . I knew better. Been there and done that—it doesn't work.

Please hear me with your heart. You are on the top of God's priority list. God hates divorce. When a marriage is dissolved, a covenant with God is broken, but God will not break His covenant with you. Never forget that.

When a father abandons a child, God draws closer. He will provide the male role models your son needs and the male father figures your daughter needs. When a child is abandoned by a mother, God draws closer. He will provide the female role models your daughter needs and the female mother figures your son needs.

Hold your head high, and allow these words from Psalm 34:3–4 to penetrate your heart and give you comfort: "I sought the Lord, and he answered me; he delivered me from all my fears. Those who look to him are radiant; their faces are never covered with shame."

He did it for me; He wants to do it for you. Just ask. He's waiting to deliver you so you can lead His children back to Him.

This revised edition of *Raising Respectful Children in a Disrespectful World* would not be complete without the "rest of the story":

Two weeks before Christmas in 2009, I ordered not one, not two, but eight needlepoint stockings, each embroidered with a different name—Nick, Robert, Mary, Garett, Sally, Rich, Jack, and Burton. Nick carefully measured the living room mantel and proudly added eight stockings to Jill, Boyce, and Chad's stockings, which had been hanging every Christmas for the last fifteen years. From three to eleven stockings in one year.

Since 2009, we have added stockings for Allie and Alston. This Christmas we're adding a stocking for Elise.

This is my way of saying that God sent the most wonderful man into my life in 2008. Godly, kind, and patient, with the added bonus of being terribly handsome. No one was more surprised than I was.

I wasn't looking. I wasn't hoping. I wasn't lonely. I was satisfied.

Satisfied, you're asking? How was I satisfied with a life that did not include a soul mate? A dear friend sent me a poem after my first husband left home, written in the 1200s by a Catholic monk who died at the tender age of thirty-six. This young man had found an intimacy with God that we too often seek to find in a human relationship. I hope you will take his words to heart, as I did:

Be Satisfied with Me
by St. Anthony of Padua

Everyone longs to give themselves completely to someone,
To have a deep soul relationship with another,
To be loved thoroughly and exclusively.
But to a Christian, God says, "No, not until you are satisfied,
Fulfilled and content with being loved by me alone,
With giving yourself totally and unreservedly to me,
With having an intensely personal
and unique relationship with me alone,
Discovering that only in me is your satisfaction to be found,
Will you be capable of the perfect human relationship,
That I have planned for you.
You will never be united to another
Until you are united with me.
Exclusive of anyone or anything else.
Exclusive of any other desires or longings.
I want you to stop planning, to stop wishing,
and allow me to give you
The most thrilling plan existing . . . one you cannot imagine.
I want you to have the best. Please allow me to bring it to you.
You just keep watching me, expecting the greatest things.
Keep experiencing the satisfaction that I am.
Keep listening and learning the things that I tell you.
Just wait, that's all. Don't be anxious, don't worry.
Don't look around at things others have gotten

Or that I have given them.
Don't look around at the things you think you want,
Just keep looking off and away up to me,
Or you'll miss what I want to show you.
And then, when you're ready, I'll surprise you with a love
Far more wonderful than you could dream of.
You see, until you are ready,
and until the one I have for you is ready,
I am working even at this moment
To have both of you ready at the same time.
Until you are both satisfied exclusively with me.
The world tells us we have to love ourselves
before someone else will love us. Not true.
We don't need to love ourselves more, we need to love Him more.
We need to accept His love for us and love Him in return.

I remember sitting in my chair in the living room one Christmas morning more than ten years ago looking at those three stockings, reminiscing about days long past. After years of heartache and longing, rather than feeling abandoned, I felt loved. I had found the contentment of being satisfied with Him, and no other. A love like no other. An acceptance like no other.

In God's perfect timing, when I least expected it, He sent Nick into my life to be His eyes of mercy looking at me in the morning and His arms of comfort wrapped around me at night. The least deserving I was, but surely, the most grateful.

My advice? Don't look around, look up.

Appendix B

Family Protection Policy

LET ME ENCOURAGE you to pray this prayer, based on Ephesians 6, each morning for your family. Following the example given in Scripture, "the two shall become one," if you are praying this as husband and wife, there is great symbolism in using the plural pronouns with the singular nouns. For instance, "upon *our head*," represents the solidarity that takes place within marriage. If you are praying this as a single parent (as I did for many years) use the singular throughout. For instance, "upon *my head*." Praying God's Word back to Him invokes powerful protection for your family.

Family Protection Prayer

Lord, place upon our head the helmet of salvation,
To protect our mind.
Place upon our chest the breastplate of righteousness,
To protect our heart.

Buckle around us the belt of Truth,
That we would know the Truth and speak the Truth,
That we would not be deceived, nor would we deceive.
Lord, we will carry the sword of the Spirit,
Your Word, as an offensive weapon.
Enable us to walk in the path of peace
You lay before us this day,
Not stepping to the left or to the right,
But walking in its narrow way.
And now, with the Holy Spirit dwelling within,
With Jesus Christ, our brother, standing with us,
And with the Lord God Almighty empowering us,
We will stand and hold the shield of faith this day
for (<u>your children's names</u>),
Until each can carry it in their own faith.
Amen.

Appendix C

After the Storm

A S YOU KNOW by now, Katrina changed Louisiana forever. We have experienced many storms since, but none have had the impact on us that she did.

Just two months after Katrina, one of my dearest friends, Dr. Jean Rohloff, an English professor at Louisiana State University, wrote the following poem acknowledging the destruction left behind, while pointing us to the only One who can enable us to stand after the storm. I pray her words will give you encouragement as you help your children after the storm.

After the Storm
by Jean Rohloff

Hear the howling of the winds. Hear the roaring of the seas.
Feel the quaking of the earth. See the breaking of the trees.
The sky is filled with darkness. Our hearts are filled with fear.

But through the raging tempest, oh, God, we know You are near.
After the storm You turn the seas to dry land.
After the storm You lift us up so we can stand.
We walk into the sun, in the light of the Holy One.
Into Your arms we run, after the storm.
And though there is destruction in the wind and the flood,
Our souls are secure in You by Your cleansing blood.
You are our mighty fortress. You are our hiding place.
You lead us to the rock by Your amazing grace!

Appendix D

Must-Read Books for Parents

Dietrich Bonhoffer, *The Cost of Discipleship*

S. Truett Cathy, *It's Better to Build Boys Than Mend Men*

Henry Cloud, *Boundaries* series

——, *Changes That Heal*

Kara Durbin, *Parenting with Scripture: A Topical Guide for Teachable Moments*

John Eldredge, *Waking the Dead: The Glory of a Heart Fully Alive*

——, *Wild at Heart: Discovering the Secret of a Man's Soul* (for dads)

John & Staci Eldredge, *Captivating: Unveiling the Mystery of a Woman's Soul* (for moms)

Elisabeth Elliot, *Discipline: The Glad Surrender*

Richard J. Foster, *Devotional Classics: Selected Readings for Individuals and Groups*

Sharon Jaynes, *Being a Great Mom, Raising Great Kids*

Ellie Kay, *Money Doesn't Grow on Trees: Teaching Kids the Value of a Buck*

Timothy Keller, *Counterfeit Gods: The Empty Promises of Money, Sex, and Power, and the Only Hope that Matters*

——, *The Freedom of Self-Forgetfulness*

——, *The Meaning of Marriage: Facing the Complexities of Commitment with the Wisdom of God*

Thomas A. Kempis, *The Imitation of Christ*

Brother Lawrence, *The Practice of the Presence of God with Spiritual Maxims*

Kevin Leman, Dr., *When Your Best Isn't Good Enough*

——, *Sex Begins in the Kitchen: Because Love Is an All-Day Affair*

C. S. Lewis, *The Chronicles of Narnia* series

——, *The Screwtape Letters*

——, *Surprised by Joy: The Shape of My Early Life*

Max Lucado, *It's Not about Me: Rescue from the Life We Thought Would Make Us Happy*

Brennan Manning, *The Ragamuffin Gospel*

Calvin Miller, *Into the Depths of God: Where Eyes See the Invisible, Ears Wear the Inaudible, and Minds Conceive the Inconceivable*

Kathy Collard Miller, *When Counting to Ten Isn't Enough: A Strategy for Confident Parenting*

Walker Moore, *Rite of Passage Parenting: Four Essential Experiences to Equip Your Kids for Life*

John Ortberg, *The Life You've Always Wanted*

——, *When the Game Is Over, It All Goes Back in the Box*

Jolene Philo, *Different Dream Parenting: A Practical Guide to Raising a Child with Special Needs*

Jill Rigby, *Manners of the Heart Elementary Character Education Curriculum*

——, *Raising Unselfish Children in a Self-Absorbed World*

Linda W. Rooks, *Broken Heart on Hold: Surviving Separation*

John Rosemond, *John Rosemond's New Parent Power*

——, *Parenting by the Book: Biblical Wisdom for Raising Your Child*

Kendra Smiley with John Smiley, *Do Your Kids a Favor . . . Love Your Spouse*

——, *Be the Parent: Seven Choices You Can Make to Raise Great Kids*

Hannah Whitall Smith, *The Christian's Secret of a Happy Life*

Vicki Tiedi, *Parenting on Your Knees: Prayers and Practical Guidance for the Preschool Years*

J.R.R. Tolkien, *Lord of the Rings*

A. W. Tozer, *Keys to the Deeper Life*

——, *The Knowledge of the Holy*

——, *The Pursuit of God*

Dallas Willard, *Hearing God: Developing a Conversational Relationship with God*

——, *Renovation of the Heart: Putting on the Character of Christ*

Notes

S CRIPTURE QUOTATIONS NOT otherwise marked are taken from the Holy Bible, *New International Version*®. Scripture quotations marked KJV are taken from the *King James Version*®. Scripture quotations marked MSG are taken from *The Message*®. Scriptures marked NKJV are taken from the *New King James Version*®. Scriptures marked CEV are taken from the *Contemporary English Version*®. Scriptures marked NASB are taken from the *New American Standard Bible*®.

Chapter 1: What Went Wrong?

1. CBS Los Angeles, "Study Finds More Baby Boomers Getting Divorced in Their 50s," June 12, 2012, http://losangeles.cbslocal.com/2012/06/12/study-finds-divorce-rate-soaring-among-baby-boomers/ (accessed September 13, 2012).

2. Jean M. Twenge and W. Keith Campbell, *The Narcissism Epidemic: Living in the Age of Entitlement* (New York: Free Press/ Division of Simon & Schuster, 2009), 9.

3. John Rosemond, "From Spock to Rosemond," syndicated column, July 25, 2000. From author's files.

4. Interview with Roy F. Baumeister, Florida State University, http://www.fsu.edu/profiles/ baumeister/ (accessed October 4, 2012).

5. Judith Martin, "The World's Oldest Virtue," *First Things* 33 (May 1993): 22–25.

6. Luke 6:45.

7. Luke 6:45 CEV.

8. Luke 6:45 MSG.

9. See John 17:15.

Chapter 2: Where Have All the Parents Gone?

1. CBS News, "All Missing Hurricane Kids Found," February 11, 2009, http://www.cbsnews. com/2100-500487_162-1430442 .html (accessed August 1, 2012).

2. David Brooks, "The Organization Kid," *Atlantic Monthly*, April 2001, http://www.theatlantic.com (accessed October 4, 2012).

3. Camilla A. Herrera, "Too Much Parenting Might Be Damaging," *Stamford Advocate*, July 23, 2005.

4. Marjorie Coeyman, "Childhood Achievement Test," *Christian Science Monitor*, December 17, 2002, http://www.csmonitor.com/2002/1217/p11s02-lehl.html (accessed October 4, 2012).

5. Camilla A. Herrera, "For 'Alpha Parents' Only the Best Will Do," *Stamford Advocate*, July 18, 2005.

6. Nancy Gibbs, "Do Kids Have Too Much Power?" July 17–18, 2001, http://www.time.com/time/world/article/0,8599,2047876,00.html (accessed October 4, 2012).

7. Krista Conger, "TV in Bedrooms Linked to Lower Test Scores," *Stanford Report*, July 13, 2005, http://news-service.stanford.edu/news/2005/july13/med-tv-071305.html (accessed April 13, 2006).

8. Common Sense Media, "Zero to Eight: Children's Media Use in America," October 25, 2011, http://www.commonsensemedia.org/sites/default/files/research/zerotoeightfinal2011.pdf (accessed August 9, 2012).

9. Will Edwards, "The 7 Habits," http://www.whitedovebooks.co.uk/7-habits/7-habits.htm (accessed October 4, 2012).

10. Matthew 5:36–37.

11. Quotations Page, http://www.quotationspage.com/quote/30186.html (accessed October 4, 2012).

Chapter 3: Enroll in the School of Respect

1. Proverbs 22:6.

2. James Strong, *The Exhaustive Concordance of the Bible: Showing Every Word of the Text of the Common English Version of the Canonical Books, and Every Occurrence of Each Word in Regular Order*, electronic ed. (Ontario: Woodside Bible Fellowship, 1996), 2596.

3. Strong, *Exhaustive Concordance*, 1870.

4. Noah Webster's 1828 Dictionary.

5. Dr. Alberta Siegel, professor of psychology at Stanford University. *Stanford Observer*, October 1973, 4.

6. Deuteronomy 4:9.

7. George Bernard Shaw, www.thinkexist.com.

8. Michael Resnick et al., "Protecting Adolescents from Harm," Findings from the National Longitudinal Study on Adolescent Health, *Journal of the American Medical Association* 278, no. 10 (September 10, 1997), http://jama.ama-assn.org/cgi/content/abstract/278/10/823?maxtoshow=&HITS=10&hits=10&RESULTFORMAT=&fulltext=%22protecting+adolescents+from+harm%22&searchid=1139432338669_8489&FIRSTINDEX=0&journalcode=jama (accessed October 4, 2012).

9. Michael Resnick, interview by Norman Swan, "Adolescent Health," The Health Report: ABC Radio National, September 22, 1997.

10. Larry Crabb, *Connecting* (Nashville, Tenn.: Word, 1997).

11. Henry Ward Beecher, http://www.quotationpark.com/topics/children.html (accessed October 4, 2012).

Chapter 4: Stress Purpose, Not Performance

1. NOAA, "Muppets Go Flying with NOAA's Hurricane Hunter Aircraft," July 19, 2012, http://celebrating200years.noaa.gov/magazine/muppets/welcome.html.

2. NBC6, Edward Colby, "Flying through Severe Weather Is Hurricane Hunter's Job," June 20, 2012, http://www.nbcmiami.com/news/local/Flying-Through-Severe-Weather-Is-Hurricane-Hunters-Job-160876145.html.

3. Janine Bempechat, "Helping Children Be Their Best," http://www.pta.org/2530.htm (accessed October 4, 2012).

4. Michelle Kees, "Is Your Child Overscheduled and Overstressed?" *Children's Mental Health News*, July 29, 2005.

5. Luke 22:42 KJV.

6. Robin Fambrough, *The Advocate*, "Episcopal's Claney Duplechin wins national award," June 26, 2012, http://theadvocate.com/sports/preps/3192108-123/episcopal-track-coach-claney-duplechin (accessed September 22, 2012).

7. Ibid.

8. ThinkExist.com, http://en.thinkexist.com/quotes/zig_ziglar/3.html (accessed October 4, 2012).

9. *American Heritage Dictionary*, s.v. "perseverance."

Chapter 5: Coach; Don't Cheerlead

1. *Coast Guard Compass,* "Reflections on Katrina—MK1 Young and ME2 Watson," http://coastguard.dodlive.mil/2010/08/reflections-on-katrina-mk1-young-me1-watson/.

2. Jean Twenge, L. Zhang, and C. Im, "It's Beyond My Control: A Cross-temporal Meta-analysis of Increasing Externality in Locus of Control, 1960–2002," *Personality and Social Psychology Review* 8 (2004): 308–19.

3. Mike Tymn, "Third Wind," *National Masters News,* February 2005, http://fairmodel.econ.yale.edu/aging/tymn.pdf, accessed October 4, 2012.

4. John B. Scott and James S. Ward, *Champions for Life* (Columbus, Ohio: Nicholas Ward, 2004), 166.

5. Thomas Edison Quotes, http://www.brainyquote.com/quotes/authors/t/thomas_a_edison.html (accessed October 4, 2012).

6. "Landry Remembered at Services," CBS News, http://www.cbsnews.com/stories/2000/02/17/archive/main161898.shtml (accessed October 4, 2012).

7. Matthew 7: 24–25.

8. Ephesians 4:14, italics mine.

9. Coaching Quotes, http://www.coachqte.com/landry.html (accessed October 4, 2012).

10. John B. Scott and James S. Ward, *Champions for Life* (Columbus, Ohio: Nicholas Ward, 2004), 166.

Chapter 6: Set Boundaries Without Building Walls

1. "Cumulonimbus Mammatus," http://weatherwing.com/Cumu lonimbus-Mammatus.html.

2. "Mammatus cloud," http://en.wikipedia.org/wiki/Mammatus_cloud.

3. Gary Ezzo and Robert Bucknam, *On Becoming Pre-Toddlerwise: From Babyhood to Toddlerhood* (New York: Parent-Wise Solutions, Inc., 2009), 93.

4. Genesis 3:8.

5. Robert Fulghum, *All I Really Need to Know I Learned in Kindergarten* (New York: Villard, 1990), 6.

6. John 15:15.

Chapter 7: Use Discipline, Not Punishment

1. Max Bazerman and Michael Watkins, *Predictable Surprises: The Disasters You Should Have Seen Coming, and How to Prevent Them* (Watertown, Mass: Harvard Business Review Press, 2004), 6.

2. Hebrews 12:11.

3. *Merriam-Webster* OnLine, http://www.m-w.com/dictionary/di scipline (accessed April 13, 2006).

4. *Webster's Desk Dictionary*, 1995, s.v. "punishment."

5. Ephesians 6:4, italics mine.

6. Hebrews 12:11.

7. 1 Timothy 1:5 NASB.

8. Psalm 139:23–24, italics mine.

9. Proverbs 6:23.

Chapter 8: Shield Your Treasures from the Trash: *Magazines, Books, and Music*

1. "Army Corps of Engineers: History of the Lake Pontchartrain and Vicinity Hurricane Protection Project" (General Accountability Office, November 2005), http://www.gao.gov/new .items/d06244t.pdf (accessed on August 29, 2012).

2. Corrie ten Boom, *The Hiding Place* (Uhrichsville, Ohio: Barbour, 1971).

3. Media Awareness Network, "How Marketers Target Kids," http://www.media-awareness.ca/english/parents/marketing/marketers_target_kids.cfm (accessed April 13, 2006).

4. Fox News, "Victoria Hearst Says Her Family's Cosmopolitan Magazine 'Pornographic,' Joins Campaign to Get It Brown Bagged," September 7, 2012, http://www.foxnews.com/enter tainment/2012/09/06/victoria-hearst-says-her-family-cosmo politan-magazine-pornographic-joins/#ixzz26lv5O8cm.

5. Cecily von Ziegesar, *Gossip Girl* (New York: Little, Brown, 2002), 3.

6. Lesley Blume, *Huffpost Healthy Living*, "15 Going on 50: How Gossip Girl Is Killing Youth Culture," October 24, 2007,

http://www.huffingtonpost.com/lesley-m-m-blume/ 15-going
-on-50-how-gossip_b_69691.html?view=print&comm_ref=
false (accessed September 2, 2012).

7. Sarah Webb Quest, "The Gossip Girl Speaks," October 17,
2004, http://www.suite101.com/article.cfm/professional_writ
ing/111559 (accessed April 13, 2006).

8. Sally Lodge, "Gossip Girl Returns—with a Vengeance," *Publishers Weekly*, February 3, 2011, http://www.publishersweekly
.com/pw/by-topic/childrens/childrens-book-news/article/
45994-gossip-girl-returns-with-a-vengeance.html.

9. Ibid.

10. James C. Humes, *Speaker's Treasury of Anecdotes about the Famous* (New York: Harper & Row, 1978), 154.

11. WLOX 13 News, "'Gossip Girls' books banned from Picayune
schools," September 20, 2011, http://www.wlox.com/story/
15510671/gossip-girls-books-banned-from-picayune-schools.

12. Answers.com, "Parents Music Resource Center," http://www
.answers.com/topic/parents-music-resource-center (accessed October 4, 2012).

13. 1 John 2:16–17.

14. Proverbs 19:21.

15. Jeremiah 29:11.

16. Romans 16:17–19.

17. Philippians 4:8.

Chapter 9: Shield Your Treasures from the Trash:
Movies, TV, Video Games, and the Internet

1. Do Something.org, "11 Facts About Hurricane Katrina," http://www.dosomething.org/tipsandtools/11-facts-about-hurricane-katrina (accessed October 4, 2012).

2. Brian Handwerk, "New Orleans Levees Not Built for Worst Case Events," *National Geographic News*, September 5, 2005, http://news.nationalgeographic.com/news/pdf/14919583.html.

3. Ibid.

4. Larry Irons, "Homeland Security Affairs," Volume I, Issue 2, 2005, http://www,hsaj.org.

5. BBC News, "New Star Wars Movie a Bloodbath," May 4, 2005, http://news.bbc.co.uk/2/hi/entertainment/4513837.stm (accessed April 13, 2006).

6. Kimberly Thompson, "Violence, Sex, and Profanity in Films: Correlation of Movie Ratings with Content," *Medscape General Medicine*, July 2004, http://www.medscape.com/viewarticle/505766.

7. Fox News, "New Study Says Full-Frontal Nudity on Prime-Time TV Up 6,300 Percent Over Last Year," http://www.foxnews.com/entertainment/2012/08/23/new-study-says-full-frontal-nudity-on-prime-time-tv-up-400-over-last-year/ (accessed August 14, 2012).

8. Ibid.

9. David Bauder, "Raunch Meter Rises for CBS Monday Comedies," January 23, 2012, http://finance.yahoo.com/news Raunch-meter-rises-CBS-Monday-apf-1616847455.html.

10. Ibid.

11. Parents Television Council, "Reality on MTV: Gender Portrayals on MTV, Reality Programming," http://www.parentstv.org/PTC/publications/reports/MTV-RealityStudy/MTV-Reality Study_Dec11.pdf (accessed August 13, 2012).

12. *Frontline*, May 24, 2004, http://www.pbs.org/wgbh/pages front line/shows/music/interviews/ (accessed April 13, 2006).

13. The Kaiser Family Foundation, "Generation M2: Media in the Lives of 8- to 18-Year-Olds," January 1, 2010, http://www.kff .org/entmedia/upload/8010.pdf.

14. S. R. Lichter, *Sexual Imagery in Pop Culture* (Washington, D.C. Center for Media and Popular Policy, 2000).

15. American Psychiatric Association report, 2004.

16. Forbes, "Riot Games' League of Legends Officially Becomes Most Played PC Game in the World," July 11, 2012, http://www.forbes.com/sites/johngaudiosi/ 2012/07/11/riot-games-league-of-legends-officially-becomes-most-played-pc-game-in-the-world/print/.

17. Rebecca L. Collins et al., "Watching Sex on Television Predicts Adolescent Initiation of Sexual Behavior," *Pediatrics* 114, no. 3 (2004): 280–89.

18. Common Sense Media, "Zero to Eight: Children's Media Use in

America," October 15, 2011, http://www.commonsensemedia
.org/research/zero-eight-childrens-media-use-america/key
-finding-3%3A-kids-under-2-spend-most-time-watching-tv.

19. Ibid.

20. Dimitri A. Christakis et al., "Early Television Exposure and
Subsequent Attentional Problems in Children," *Pediatrics* 113
(2004): 708–13.

21. Pew Research Center, "Support for Tougher Indecency Measures, but Worries about Government Intrusiveness," April 19,
2005.

22. *Time* magazine poll, March 3, 2005.

23. Federal Communications Commission, http://www.fcc.gov/.

24. C. R. Jayachandran, "Porn Rules Net Revenue Charts," Times
News Network, September 26, 2003. Accessed online at
http://economictimes.indiatimes.com/articleshow/msid-
203421.

25. Jerry Ropelato, "Internet Pornography Statistics," http://inter
net-filter-review.toptenreviews.com/internet-pornography
-statistics-pg5.html (accessed January 17, 2013).

26. Neil Postman, *The Disappearance of Childhood* (New York:
Delacorte, 1982).

27. As reported by CBS News on May 2, 2002. For more information on the full report, "Youth, Pornography, and the Internet,"
from the National Research Council, visit www.nationalacade-
mies.org.

28. Kelly Patricia O'Meara, "Free Speech Trumps 'Virtual' Child Porn," *Insight on the News*, May 27, 2002.

29. Pew Research Center, "Teens, Kindness, and Cruelty on Social Network Sites," November 9, 2011, http://pewinternet.org /Reports/2011/Teens-and-social-media/Summary/Findings .aspx. (accessed September 16, 2012).

30. Common Sense Media, "Social Media, Social Life: How Teens View Their Digital Lives," June 26, 2012, http://commonsense media.org/research/social-media-social-life/key-finding-3%3A -most-teens-prefer-face-to-face-communication.

31. Ibid.

32. Intel, "2011 State of Mobile Etiquette," http://newsroom.intel. com/docs/DOC-1883.

33. Suzanne Choney, "52 percent of kids under age 8 have access to mobile media," http://www.nbcnews.com/technology/52-per cent-kids-under-age-8-have-access-mobile-media-119492.

34. Pew Research Center, "Teens, Smartphones, and Texting," March 19, 2012, http://pewinternet.org/Reports/2-12/Teens -and-smartphones.aspx.

35. Ibid.

36. Susan Murray, "A Disrespectful Culture," Answers for Me, 2009, http://www.answersforme.org/article/82/find-answers/ children/a-disrespectful-culture (accessed September 18, 2012).

37. Growing Wireless, "CITA—The Wireless Association and The Wireless Foundation Launch Growing Wireless Campaign

and Website to Help Parents Teach Their Kids How to Use Wireless Responsibly," http://www.growingwireless.com/media -center/press-releases (accessed September 12, 2012).

Chapter 10: Engage; Don't Entertain

1. ThinkExist.com, http://thinkexist.com/quotation/first_comes _thought-then_organization_of_that/294540.html.

2. *Merriam-Webster's Desk Dictionary*, 1995, s.v. "imagination."

3. ThinkExist.com, http://en.thinkexist.com/quotation/imaginat ion_is_more_important_than_knowledge/145946.html

4. Fred Rogers, *The World According to Mister Rogers* (New York: Hyperion, 2003), 183.

Chapter 11: Teach Gratefulness, Not Greediness

1. TimeMoneyland, "We've Spent Almost $6 Billion on iPhone Repairs Since 2007," September 20, 2012, http://moneyland .time.com/2012/09/20/weve-spent-almost-6-billion-on-iphone-repairs-since-2007/ (accessed September 22, 2012).

2. ABC News, "Today's Teens More Anxious, Depressed, and Paranoid Than Ever," December 10, 2009, http://abcnews.go.com /Health/MindMoodNews/todays-teens-anxious-depressed -paranoid/story?id=9281013, (accessed October 4, 2012).

3. Parent page, "Blow up Your TV!??" http://www.lausd.k12.ca.us/

Haskell_EL/parent%20 information/tv2.htm (accessed April 13, 2006).

4. John Austin, "Americans' race for space fuels boom in self-storage," *Advocate*, November 13, 2005, H1.

5. Ibid.

6. Mark 8:36–37.

7. See Acts 20:35.

8. Proverbs 15:13.

Chapter 12: Listen to the Children

1. *Kramer vs. Kramer*, DVD, directed by Robert Benton (1979, Columbia Pictures Home Entertainment, 2001).

Small Group Study Guide

1. *Merriam-Webster's Desk Dictionary*, 1995, s.v. "parent."

2. Afterhours Inspirational Stories, "I Want to Be Possible," found online at http://www.inspirationalstories.com/2/264.html.

3. Heart Foundation, Australia, "Tips on Setting Unplug + Play Rules," http://www.heart.foundation.org.au/SiteCollection Documents/Healthy%20Kids%20-%20Tips%20on%20set ting%20unplug%20and%20play%20rules.pdf.

Jill Rigby Garner

Speaker, Author, and Parenting Expert

About the Author

J ILL RIGBY GARNER, character education and parenting expert, nonprofit founder of Baton Rouge-based Manners of the Heart®, is also an inspiring speaker, award-winning author, and the publisher of heart education programs and books for students, educators, and parents. A popular media guest, Garner has appeared on the CBS *Early Show*; CNN; *Focus on the Family*; *Family Life Today*; a monthly parenting segment on local WAFB; and more than 350 radio shows across the country. She is a member of AWSA (Advanced Writers and Speakers Association); founding board member of the Louisiana Family Forum, an organization committed to defending faith, freedom, and the traditional family; and an advisory board member of Dream Teachers, recognizing educators and inspiring excellence in the education profession. Most recently, she participated as one of twelve experts in an online global parenting summit, through the innovative FLOW platform out of Singapore. Jill's deepest desire and calling are to bring a return of God's principles of respect and civility to our society. Readers and listeners, alike are motivated to action through Jill's contagious passion that fosters transformative change.

MANNERS *of the* HEART®

Manners of the Heart® is a non-profit organization working to create a more positive moral culture and bring back respect, responsibility and civility to our society. At Manners of the Heart®, we are dedicated to transforming homes, schools and communities through instructional programs designed to build character, strengthen morals and increase respectfulness among children and adults. This character education, referred to as "Heart Education," is the training of the next generation to have not only head knowledge to lead, but heart knowledge to lead in the right direction.

MANNERS *of the* **HEART**®
215 Royal Street
Baton Rouge, Louisiana 70802
(225) 383-3235
www.mannersoftheheart.org

www.mannersoftheheart.org

Without respect...
children cannot learn.

Embark on an adventure to the picturesque town of Merryville where Wise Ol' Wilbur the owl lives in the enchanted Happle Tree. Children enjoy learning about respect and manners with help from Merryville's delightful characters such as Billy Bee Right, Buddy and Bully bulldogs, Sketch the skunk, and twin raccoons Peter and Penelope. Join good-hearted Tommy Tripper as he encounters real-life problems and faces challenging situations that require tough decision-making.

www.mannersoftheheart.org